Skateboarding

Past — Present — Future

Rhyn Noll

Schiffer Publishing Ltd®
4880 Lower Valley Road, Atglen, PA 19310 USA

Dedication

This book is dedicated to all the skaters who kept skating even after they purchased their first car.

I also dedicate this book to the skaters and historians who were forthcoming with history, stories, and materials. Jim O'Mahoney, Jim Phillips, Todd Huber, Dale Smith, and Ed Economy all contributed to a clear picture for the generations ahead to see.

I thank the companies Santa Cruz Skateboards, NHS, Natural Koncepts, and Gravity and their leaders Rich Novak and Keith and Michael Bream. They have the foresight and a love for the sport that you don't see every day. These companies lead the pack in "soul." My dedication is to them and all the people who have sacrificed to tell the story.

Cover:
Exploding off the half pipe in Grant's Pass, Nathan D. *Photo R. Noll. Courtesy Jailhouse.*

Title Page:
Some of the Jailhouse Crescent City team practicing kick flips. *Photo R. Noll. Courtesy Jailhouse.*

Library of Congress Cataloging-in-Publication Data

Noll, Rhyn.
Skateboarding : past-present-future / by Rhyn Noll.
p. cm.
Summary: Provides an overview of the history of skateboarding and profiles of some of America's most famous skateboarders.
ISBN 0-7643-1845-4 (pbk.)
1. Skateboarding--United States--History--Juvenile literature. [1. Skateboarding. 2. Skateboarders.] I. Title.
GV859.8 .N32 2003
796.22--dc21

2003009359

Designed by Mark David Bowyer
Type set in Zurich BT bold italic/Dutch801 Rm BT

ISBN: 0-7643-1845-4
Printed in China

Published by Schiffer Publishing Ltd.
4880 Lower Valley Road
Atglen, PA 19310
Phone: (610) 593-1777; Fax: (610) 593-2002
E-mail: Schifferbk@aol.com
Please visit our web site catalog at **www.schifferbooks.com**
We are always looking for people to write books on new and related subjects. If you have an idea for a book, please contact us at the above address.

This book may be purchased from the publisher.
Include $3.95 for shipping. Please try your bookstore first.
You may write for a free catalog.

In Europe, Schiffer books are distributed by
Bushwood Books
6 Marksbury Ave. Kew Gardens
Surrey TW9 4JF England
Phone: 44 (0)20 8392-8585; Fax: 44 (0)20 8392-9876
E-mail: Bushwd@aol.com
Free postage in the UK. Europe: air mail at cost.
Please try your bookstore first.

Contents

Acknowledgements

Beverly Noll
Bettie Roberts
Sarah Noll, editor
Remy Noll, associate editor
Dane Noll
Bills Wheels
Randal Fuller
Dale Smith

Ed Economy
Todd Huber of Skatelab
Richard Barnick of Tsunami Surf & Sport
Roy Gonzalas
Cleave Gardner
Jean Cooper
Buddy Carr of Tracker Trucks

Liz Barbee
Leroy Granis
Jim Noll
Atilla Azsodi, associate photo editor
Michael Breem of Gravity
Brad Edwards
Rich Novak of NHS Skateboards

Jim Phillips
ET Surf and Skate
Just Long Boards
Streetsurfer™
Jail House™
Greg Noll
Jim O'Mahoney
Carrasco family

Remy Noll stylin' with an ominous sky overhead. *Photo R. Noll Courtesy Streetsurfer*

Preface

The truth is rarely pure and never simple, and being an honest broker of information isn't always easy. My goal has been to document the sport of skateboarding. I will share some of what I have learned about the history of skateboarding with you.

A lifetime of skating has led me to you. When I was growing up, I saw and heard about a few bold souls who made a huge impact on other people's lives. I felt compelled to act, to make a difference, and to affect others in a positive way. This would be something. I am not talking about big things, just small things, maybe getting someone to ride who hadn't skated until they read my first book (*Skateboard Retrospective*) or bringing pride to the great legacy of skateboarding.

I have written this for your children and your children's children. I have tried to bring some of the facts of skateboarding together to make a clear picture for history and what we don't know about each other. I hope to give you the common ground that skateboards provide. It is a strong legacy and one to be proud of.

Dane Noll out for an evening cruise. *Photo R. Noll. Courtesy Jailhouse*

Chapter 1

Making History

The best way to predict the future is to create it yourself. To me, skateboarding is like a math problem: you work on it, and work on it, until you solve it.

One thing about surfers and their need to skate: skating usually comes secondary to surfing. I think, over the years, that fact became resented by skaters who did not know how to surf. Eventually, in the 1980s, skaters who didn't surf split off and began to change skateboarding forever. Surfing and skateboarding lost their practicality over the years for high performance. For example, kids who ride a short surfboard today don't care that the board does not even float their body weight. They sacrifice that for the higher power of radical maneuverability, the ability to do the most insane stunts. But is it worth it?

Skateboarding is almost like a mirror-image of surfing. Once the boards got to a certain point, they went as far as it seemed they could with today's technology. As high performance as they could possibly be, they became as small and as light and as narrow as they could be. They push the envelope for almost every category. What I appreciate, again and again, in the skateboard industry as in the surf industry, is when people stepped back and said, "Wait a minute," which is not always the popular thing to do. They say, "This board isn't floating properly anymore, it isn't gliding properly or it doesn't ride the street anymore." The riders have stepped back from that brink and said, "Wait a minute, what happened to the practical stuff? Not everybody is a *&#@* pro, not everybody gets six or seven foot airs, not everybody that surfs wants to thrash. Some people like to nose ride, some people like to have smooth travel and the glide of a more practical board. Some people like to have the wave-catching ability of a bigger board."

Skateboarding is the same thing. The boards are pushed to the limit until they are really not a practical board anymore. Now they have become a tool to do the most extreme tricks of the trade. That is part of the sport, it's where skateboarding is as a sport, but is it practical? That's not to say that these high performance boards are not finely tuned for their environment, whatever it may be: a pipe or the bowl at the skate park. These boards are built for these surfaces for sure. Skateboarding has reached a peak as far as the tools we use go.

What I appreciate is the fact that there are so many choices now. If you're a skater or a surfer, you are not confined to what a small group of people think is best or hottest. Another group of people said, "Hey, we want to ride too." So these different facets of skating and surfing were born. Both sports have come full circle. I have the choice to ride a '70s board or an '80s or a '90s skateboard and that's ok. I fit into the sport somewhere; I'm not excluded.

Dane Noll hanging at the harbor.
Photo R. Noll. Courtesy Jailhouse

Dane Noll Hawaiian style. *Photo R. Noll Courtesy Jailhouse*

Dane Noll. *Photo R. Noll Courtesy Jailhouse*

Dane Noll testing some new ground in Klamath Cal. *Photo R. Noll Courtesy Jailhouse*

Dane Noll though the redwoods on an all terrain board. *Photo R. Noll*

Dane chillin' at Elk Prairie, California. *Photo R. Noll. Courtesy Jailhouse*

Jacoby Larson, one of the neighborhood kids. *Photo R. Noll. Courtesy Jailhouse*

Remy Hannah floating through the leaves on a fall day. *Photo R. Noll. Courtesy Streetsurfer*

Remy Noll letting her colors fly. *Photo R. Noll. Courtesy Streetsurfer*

Remy Noll out for an evening skate while light dances on her hair, Crescent City Lighthouse. *Photo R. Noll. Courtesy Streetsurfer*

As everybody around is pushing towards this one goal of high performance, they all loose sight of the sport's roots and other facets of the sports that are just as important and fun as what they are doing now. In the search for perfection, groups tend to loose sight of practicality. When we reach that edge and then look back, it is at that moment that the pastime has truly evolved into a sport.

Form and function is the basis of what street-skaters do. If the grind doesn't have the right dynamics, it will get tried but it won't get skated. If the angle of decent is not steep enough, you cannot successfully lip-slide it. If you do not have enough speed, you won't be able to tail-slide the picnic bench. And you don't have enough height for your Nollie flip. This means you either will or won't make the staircase, risking life and limb on what seems to be the un-do-able. Pushing these boundaries is an everyday occurrence for street skaters. The un-do-able gets done. Gaps get crossed. Staircases are traversed and the hideous is conquered.

Street grind: Frank Sharp. *Photo R. Noll. Courtesy Jailhouse*

In Elsagundo, trees shoot their roots under the sidewalk and olling over the fractures is commonplace. *Photo R. Noll. Courtesy Jailhouse*

This kid was skating the Ashland park. Our youth are participating; isn't that what the Y.M.C.A has been trying to do for years? *Photo R. Noll*

James "Jimmy" doing kick flips in South Beach, Florida. *Photo John Scott. Courtesy Boris*

Dianela Bianchi, castles in the sand. *Photo John Scott. Courtesy Boris*

Nothing but stair: Nathan D. Crescent City.
Photo R. Noll. Courtesy Jailhouse

Paying most of my attention to the pros of today, instead of the legends of the past or the skaters of tomorrow, I wouldn't really have done the sport justice. To get a feel for what is happening down on the ground level of the sport, you have to go where the pros are trying to sell their boards to kids on the street and in the parks where they are skating. If you get to know the individuals, you get to know what is happening today in skating.

There seem to be three different breeds of skateboarders: park riders, street riders, and alternatives. The street skaters don't like to be called "freestyle" anymore; the cool term is "street skaters." Sure enough, this will change within the year. No matter what you call them, it is the most free style, and skaters create new moves every day.

Today, it seems that once kids reach a certain age, they become more responsible for the price of their skateboard decks. They become less interested in Pro or Signature models and more interested in thrift and practicality. These kids are skating hard and breaking boards. Mileage is a factor.

Everybody is trying to get into young peoples' heads. What's hot? Why do they like what they like? Well, they want to skate hard on equipment that is tough. Its pretty simple, as long as Mom and Dad feed them and let them go to the skate park. That's it. I know its lacking prudence, but they're just kids.

Today's successful skateboard companies aren't necessarily making just skateboards. A whole line-up of other products go along with skating. What's cool isn't about what *is* cool, it is about what's *going to be* cool. If it already *is* cool, well, then, it's no longer cool. Trying to look into the future is futile. The past might actually tell you more.

Four generations of skateboarders have made a huge impact on the sport. In 2003, skateboards are so diverse. People search for the old skate board they grew up on, in the 1960s, '70s, and '80s. That represents a lot of boards, of many different shapes and styles, from a 10"-wide kick-tail to an old fiberglass Hobie. It is now acceptable for us all to skate, and we are.

Three Revolutions

A great revolution happened in skate boarding in the mid-1970s when urethane became the preferred material for skateboard wheels. A second revolution occurred in the sport when the terms "old school" and "new school" were used to describe the separation from surf style to street style skateboarding. This happened in the 1980s. The third revolution was the widespread use of the long board, in 1996, that taped into a new nostalgia in the sport and an appreciation of the first "legends," our skateboarding forefathers.

Long boarders are the first generation to have come full circle: most either skated at one time or grew up with the sport. The fact that longboard skateboards came along in 1994 is pivotal to the fact that skateboarding was re-energized; it opened up a new market and an existing sleeping market, the "old schoolers." Skateboarders of the old school, today, should be willing to admit and be proud that "old school" riders are the basis of the sport that we know as "new school."

The "Old School" Skate Jam

The Old School Sklate Jam was like a "Who's-Who" in the skateboarding world. Everyone from Danny Bearer to Jack Smith gathered in Simi Valley, California, at Skate Lab, in 2002, to form the most amazing conglomerate of skaters ever collected.

Old School Skate Jam, Tony Alva and Wes Humpston (*Dogtown*, *Z Boys*). *Photo by and courtesy of Attila Aszodi*

The guest list included:

Jay Alabamy, Dave Duncan, Howie Idelson Everett, Steve Alba, Ed Economy, Tom Inouye Rosecrans, Ray Allen, Brad Edwards, Marty Jiminez, Kevin Rucks, Tony Alva, Eddie Elguera, Randy Katen, Billy Ruff, Kevin Anderson, Steve Ellis, Bryce Kanights, Alan Sacks, Dave Andrecht, Skip Engblom, Mitch Kaufmann, Doug Saladino, Aaron Astorga, Steve Evans, Curt Kimbell, Rod Saunders, Bob Ballou, Leilani Evans, Tom Knox, Mark Schmid, Ricky Barnes, (Kiyabu) Vinny Lopez, Paul Schmitt, Jonny Ray Bartel, Tom Fain, Alan Losi, Ben Schroeder, Kelly Belmar, Don Fischer, John Lucero, Kent Senatore, Bob Biniak, Ray Flores, Kelly Lynn, Skatemaster Neil Blender, Mike Folmer, Tony Magnusson Tate, Danielle Bostick, Scott Foss, Sean Mallard, Buck Smith, Don Bostick, Alan "Ollie" Gelfand, Dennis Martinez, Dale Smith, Dan Bourqui, Tim Marting, Jack Smith, Brian Brannon, Art Godoy, Dave "Fats," Jay Smith, Beau Brown, Steve Godoy McIntire, Marc Smith, Steve Caballero, Mark Gonzalez, Keith Meek, Mike Smith, David Carrasco, Jim Gray, Rob Mertz, C.R. Stecyk III, Rene Carrasco, Marty Grimes, Darrel Miller, Richie Carrasco, Eric "Arab" Groff, Wynn Miller, Mike Stelmasky, James Cassimus, Jeff Grosso, Muck Keith, Steve Cathey, Tommy Guerrero, Deano Mueller Stephenson, Chris Chaput, Tony Guerrero, Scott Obradovich, Chris Strople, Steve Claar, David Hackett, Peggy Oki, Tod Swank, Cliff Coleman, Omar Hassan, Steve Olson, Dave Swift, Paul Constantineau Curtis, James O'Mahoney, Ted Terrebonne, Hesselgrave Ellen, Joey Tershay, Chris Cook, Henry Hester, O'neal-Deason, Kevin Thatcher, Sam Cunningham, Lonny Hiramoto, George Orton, Jerry Valdez, Bill Danforth, Mike Hirsch, Moses Padilla, Mike Vallely Dave Dash Steve Hirsch Brian Patch Miki Vukovich, Gary "Skate" Davis, April Hoffman, Tim Payne, Bill Wahl, Stan Hoffman, Stacy Peralta, Mark Waters, Steve Day, Marc Hollander, Duane Peters, Chris Weddle, Darrel Delgado, Steve Holt, Jimmy Plumer, Cindy Whitehead, Adrian Demain, Howard Hood, Pushead Marlon, Freddie DeSoto, Rick Howard, Marty Ramos, Whitfield Art Dickey, Chuck Hults, Eddie Reatigui, George Wilson, Eric Dressen, Wes Humpston, Kevin Reed, and Chris Yandall.

Skating legend Bruce Logan, no introduction needed. *Photo by and courtesy of Attila Aszodi*

Dale Smith "Sausage Man" and Eddie "El Gato" Elguera at the Jam. *Photo by and courtesy of Attila Aszodi*

Ricky Blackheart the Old School Skate Jam. *Photo R. Noll. Courtesy Jailhouse.*

Finally a good front shot of Tony Alva, I had to earn that one. *Photo R. Noll*.

I picked up this little beauty at the OSSJ. Some say a picture is worth a thousand words. This one speaks volumes. Look at the back wheel on the board, it gives you an idea how much time this guy spends on the coping. He is blasting from one bowl to the next over the hip and he lands it smooth as silk. He is so high he is almost in the overhead lights and he is wearing a knit cap and not even breaking a sweat. Brian Patch OSSJ. *Photo R. Noll*

Dropping in at the OSSJ as he contemplates the skooter rush. *Photo R. Noll*

Eddie Elguera still laying it down. *Photo by & Courtesy of Attila Aszodi*

Chillin at the OSSJ Brian Patch , Tony Alva and Steve Olsen. *Photo by & Courtesy of Attila Aszodi*

Dino Mueller pointing out the cover which he is on.
Photo by & Courtesy of Attila Aszodi

Brian Patch. *Photo by & Courtesy of Attila Aszodi*

Cabbage with two wheels in and two wheels out, truly OldSchool in,Ocean Beach, California. *Photo Michael Bream. Courtesy Gravity*

Rider at Ashland skate park, coping grind. *Photo R. Noll*

Skate Parks

One of the things that have come out of the skate park experience for me is that youngsters amazingly show an adult etiquette. I see skaters from all eras in skate parks trading mutual respect. Skate parks are just as important to a community as a football field or a baseball field. The year 2000 marks a rebirth of skateboarding with the advent of many new skate parks and the array of new and old boards to ride. New prosperous times lie ahead for skate boarding.

Ashland skater getting ready to drop in. *Photo R. Noll*

Larry Martin with his Indie grab in Grant's Pass. *Photo R. Noll*

A brand new skate park in Brookings, Oregon. *Photo R. Noll*

Scott Star at the taco bowl in Santa Barbara. *Photo R. Noll*

Ashland, one the earliest southern Oregon skate parks. *Photo R. Noll*

Putting the Ashland park to good use. *Photo R. Noll*

Photo R. Noll

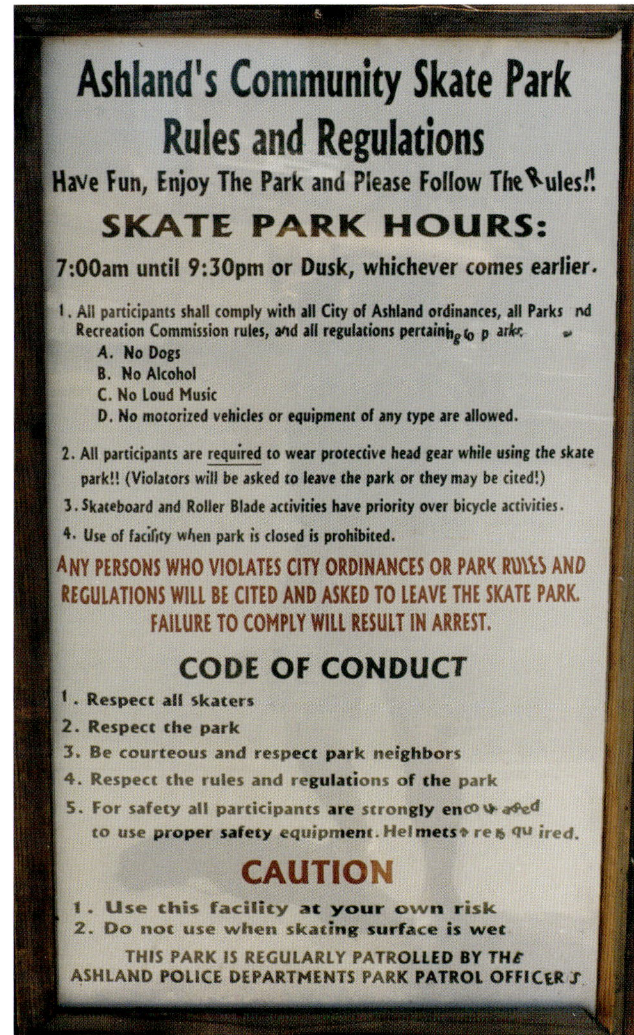

The 10 Commandments of the Ashland park. *Photo R. Noll*

Ashland park. *Photo R. Noll*

This is the deep end of the bowl in the Grant's Pass park. *Photo R. Noll*

The Medford park is the largest in southern Oregon. *Photo R. Noll*

Grant's Pass park is the best in southern Oregon. *Photo R. Noll*

I just like the way the light reflects of the concrete in the morning; it sends shivers up my spine. *Photo R. Noll*

Photo R. Noll

Medford Park

Photo R. Noll

The upper bowls in Medford are impressive but un-utilized. *Photo R. Noll*

This reflects the grief and frustration youngsters feel when their hometown is awaiting a park. *Courtesy Virgina Brubaker*

These skaters are also enjoying the obstacle in Venice. *Photo R. Noll*

Cabbage risks the elements in Japan with a fast back side carve or front side bottom turn, depending on what you're into, Converse skate park, Mt. Fuji, Japan. *Photo Michael Bream. Courtesy Gravity*

Boulder Skate Park, Boulder, Colorado. *Photo Michael Bream. Courtesy Gravity*

Scooters

Here is a case where the sport reversed itself and went back in time to its very beginning, before there was such a thing as board sports. Scooters resurfaced in a big way at the end of 2000. You could safely say just about every kid in the free world acquired a scooter by the end of 2001.

Like a ghost from the past haunting us. With it's practicality and fun, the scooter is back. Black and white is a timeless medium and it doesn't take much to imagine these kids in another time. *Photo R. Noll*

Chapter 2

1970s Flashback to the Golden Era

The fastest downhill speed is 62 mph.

What an incredible journey skateboarding has taken. From its genesis until now, it reminds me of all the great times I have had with the sport. It reminds me of my own history and legacy and makes me appreciate that I was part of elevating the sport to national enjoyment.

Skateboarding is kind of like life. It was conceived by the merging of two courageous sports: rollerskating and surfboard riding. These gave birth to skateboarding. The new sport had an infancy that was simple and very innocent, even primitive. As skateboarding grew, it also increased in coordination and strength. As it matured, new opportunities emerged. The life of the sport is evolving at an alarming rate and begins to outgrow its past equipment and ideas. It is working to create its own identity, as we all do. Sometimes, growing up, we tend to get radical, some might even say crude. Through trial and error, lessons are learned and thoughts are contemplated. Progress is made towards understanding what and who it is we are. Now, skateboarding has become something to be reckoned with. When we flex our muscles, youth's power is observed opening our minds and accepting where we have come from. We start to contemplate our future. We are integrated into society as skateboarders. It has become a family of past, present and future. We have reached adulthood.

Someday, skateboarding will be revered among all who will ever pick up a skateboard. Fathers and mothers will pass the history down with pride and a sense of attainment. The seventies, what a secret and magical time. I look back on the seventies and get melancholy. It almost seems like 100 years ago when I was there. It will live in infamy and stand the test of time as a historical hot spot. The seventies started slow still trying to recover from the sixties sting. Kids like me, we never stopped skating from the 1960's to the 1970's. It didn't matter to us kids that the sport had gone bust and was practically banned everywhere. The boys would find a way. We would piece stuff together to make our skateboards and skate them wherever we could. When I was a kid we built skateboards that emulated surfboards shapes and styles. In the 1970's I can remember swallows tails, bumps, and wingers. Impractical in function, but cool. Before that I can remember we would carpet the decks of our board for comfort and traction, you must remember this is pre-grip TaPe.

Throughout my life I have witnessed an endless amount of change in skateboarding. Throughout each of the decades of skateboarding, from clay wheels to building our own boards, we created a brand new style that was surf-orientated. Have you ever heard someone say that 80% of a vehicles ability lies in it its tires? Well the same is true for the skateboard.

When Urethane wheels rocked our world in 1970s, with unparalleled traction, it changed everything. Then Cadillac wheels urethane technology had arrived. It was like some crazy scientist somewhere concocted a wild blend of space age materials just for us skaters, at least that's how it felt as a kid back then. The truth is Urethane had been around even in the 1960s, but it just didn't get implemented, quite simply for monetary issues. Clay was cheaper and the mind set for manufacturers in the 1960's was pump it out as fast as you can because this skateboarding is just a fad and lets milk it for all its worth. This kind of short sightedness is still prevalent in the industry today and can, as you know from the '60s, ruin an industry with over- saturation. Overlooking urethane in the '60s set skateboarding back a decade.

Those crazy scientist were Bahne and Nasworthy and they changed everything. As far as I was concerned powerful turns among other things were one of the many benefits of urethane. A lot happened after that its just a blur of skating the Bowl at Riviera School and around my home up and down the street all summer long on Rivera avenue. Scattering after drop bearings in the middle of the road. So many things were going on in skateboarding at this time but I was oblivious as a kid skating in my own little surf and skate world. The endless surfing moves being performed everywhere was the focus for me. Skating was new and definitely not mainstream, yet. The same with surfing. These sports are still in their infancy and certainly a subculture not fully accepted to say the least. Many times I had to fight for my right to skate. For the most part parents wouldn't even support your skating it was a kids sport or it's a fad , they'd say.

The 1970s were rough, but fun, for me in Torrence, California. While a yodel away *Dogtowners* were making history. There was one guy named Tony Alva who caught my eye. Tony, among other surf-skaters like Buttons and Larry Bertleman, made a huge impact on my life. So, in that sense, I guess my skateboarding was influenced by *Dogtown* and the Z-Boys. In the mid-'70s, my father, Greg, moved us north to escape the rat race. Things were defiantly different up north in Crescent City, California. Let's just say some people still had a '60s mentality in the beginning of the 21st century.

The Dogtown movie was a milestone event in history. Why is it so bitchen'? Because its our history, our legacy, among many other reasons. Weather you liked the Dogtown movie or not, it brought an appreciation of the sport to the big screen. I think it is important to put Dogtown in perspective. Their story could have been a lot of kids' story in the '70s.

Downhill, Akron, Ohio. *Photo James O'Mahoney*

Rainbow Ryders & GT.
Photo James O'Mahoney

Mark Johnson in a Santa Barbara contest. *Photo James O'Mahoney*

Greg Weaver at the Long Beach Arena.
Photo James O'Mahoney

Tony Alva's wall hug. *Photo James O'Mahoney*

Steve Cathy doing a Daffy at the Long Beach Arena.
Photo James O'Mahoney

Barefoot at the Vermont drop. *Photo James O'Mahoney*

Stacy Perralta showing Henry Hester a "tailtap" up close in a runway professional contest. *Photo James O'Mahoney*

United States Skateboarding Association (USSA)-CBS Sports Free Former, the first world vertical event runway. *Photo James O'Mahoney*

George Ortin nosing 18'6" vertical runway at the USSA World Pro contest. *Photo James O'Mahoney*

Lonnie Hiramoto in a tail stall at the runway of the USSA World Pro contest. *Photo James O'Mahoney*

Christy McNichol practicing for the USSA-CBS TV Skate Challenge of the Sexes Show vs. Grizzly Adams. *Photo James O'Mahoney*

Huge USSA Skateboard Magazine skate demonstration at Anaheim Stadium with the Bahne Team *Skateboard Magazine* Team. *Photo James O'Mahoney*

Signal Hill racer. *Photo James O'Mahoney*

Tina Trefethen, the only girl ever sponsored by *Playboy* magazine, at the World Invitational in San Diego. *Photo James O'Mahoney*

Young world surfing champion Tom Curren. This was the first-ever magazine appearance of the Santa Barbara contest. *Photo James O'Mahoney*

Ellen Barryman, helmet walk, USSA-WSA New York Masters' Invitational at the Nassau Coliseum. *Photo James O'Mahoney*

Curt Lindgrin's kick-filp at the USSA Freeformer Contest, Akron, Ohio. *Photo James O'Mahoney*

Oops! Vertical fall runway. *Photo James O'Mahoney*

Hobie Team in syncronization, Anaheim, California. *Photo James O'Mahoney*

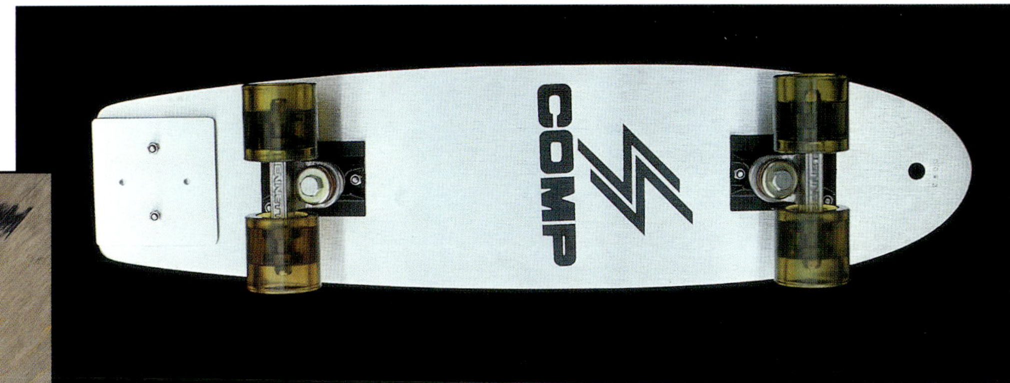

Bengal SS Competition. James O'Mahoney's design. *Photo James O'Mahoney*

Nick Valarcos, Vermont Drop. *Photo James O'Mahoney*

Andy Priciak, record longboard, 18 feet. *Photo James O'Mahoney*

Steve's Southbay with a one-wheel hang. *Photo James O'Mahoney*

One wheel. Steve's Southbay Skatepark. The best. *Photo James O'Mahoney*

Fiberflex. *Photo James O'Mahoney*

Howard Hood doing an Indy grab at Steve's Southbay. *Photo James O'Mahoney*

Bennett Pro. *Photo James O'Mahoney*

Photo James O'Mahoney

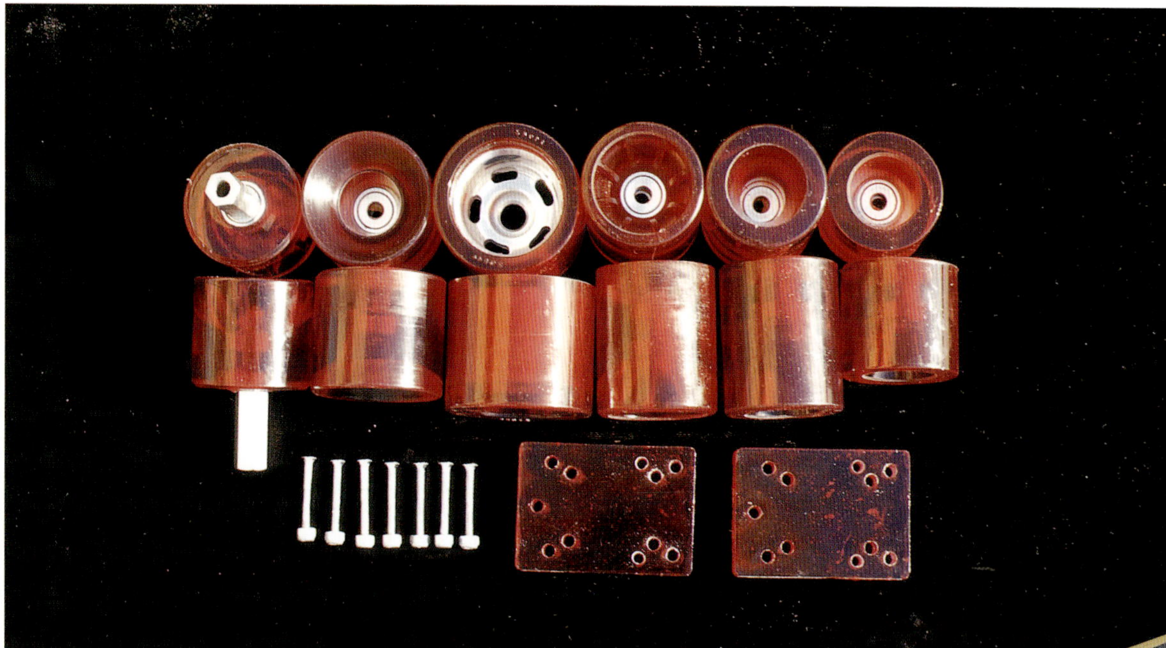

Wheels and risers. *Photo James O'Mahoney*

Skitch Hitchcock's handstand-board combo. *Photo James O'Mahoney*

Hitchcock Palm Board. *Photo James O'Mahoney*

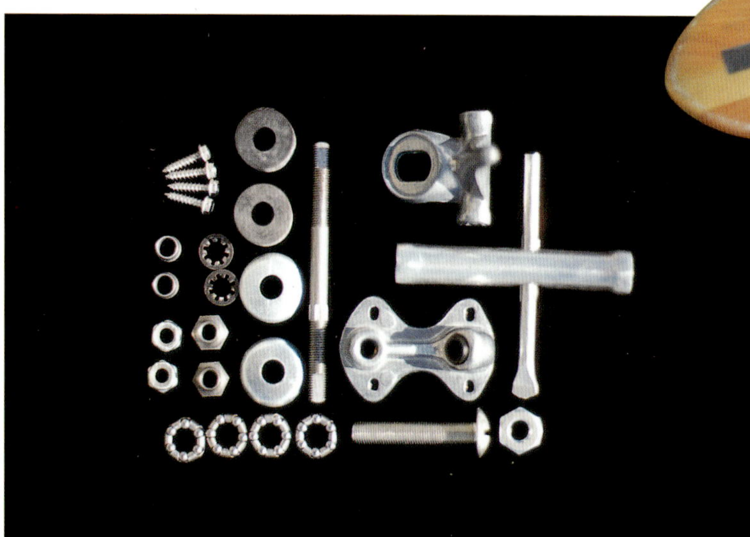

Parts. *Photo James O'Mahoney*

Laura Thornhill spins in Akron, Ohio. *Photo James O'Mahoney*

Surf skating! *Photo James O'Mahoney*

Ty Page and the Cal Jam spectacle beyond. *Photo James O'Mahoney*

Road Rider wheels advertising, 1976.
Courtesy Jim Phillips

Herbie Fletcher at Mt. Baldy pipe.
Photo James O'Mahoney

Laura Thornhill going through her routine. *Photo James O'Mahoney*

Howard Hood hangs at 9 o'clock. *Photo James O'Mahoney*

Brian Beardsley at the Akron High Jump. *Photo James O'Mahoney*

Nose Wheelie at Steve's Contest. *Photo James O'Mahoney*

Fred Flavel leaps for the Guinness Book. *Photo James O'Mahoney*

Jeff O'Mahoney's 2-board Rocket Daffy. *Photo James O'Mahoney*

Steve and Barrie Bohne Tandem Tango. *Photo James O'Mahoney*

Jeff O'Mahoney's Indy Hop. *Photo James O'Mahoney*

Hobie Orange Crate, Signal Hill. *Photo James O'Mahoney*

Girls' Downhill at Akron. *Photo James O'Mahoney*

Firestone. *Photo James O'Mahoney*

Freeformer at the Hill. *Photo James O'Mahoney*

Brian Beardsley's two-Fiat jump at Akron. *Photo James O'Mahoney*

Jim Higham the Real Bowl.

Hobie Guy. *Photo James O'Mahoney*

Skate break at Steve's Southbay. *Photo James O'Mahoney*

Steve Brown's 12-barrel launch for the Guinness Book ABC-TV meet at San Pedro, California. *Photo James O'Mahoney*

John Hutson prepares to slalom. *Photo James O'Mahoney*

Mark Bowden's 1-foot tail 360s. *Photo James O'Mahoney*

Guy Grundy and Dave Dillberg at Signal Hill. *Photo James O'Mahoney*

Guy Grundy. *Photo James O'Mahoney*

Mr. Gull Wing. *Photo James O'Mahoney*

Courtesy of Jim Phillips

Ellen O'Neil does the dance in Akron. *Photo James O'Mahoney*

A wall drop at Steve's, with Laura Thronhill watching. *Photo James O'Mahoney*

Long Beach GP demonstration Rad Ramp. *Photo James O'Mahoney*

Guy and the Infinity Stick. *Photo James O'Mahoney*

Pinks takes the Pee Wee Girls Division, Steve's Southbay. *Photo James O'Mahoney*

Grundy hits the ticker at IST Signal Hill. *Photo James O'Mahoney*

Brian Beardsley's 2-foot tail wheelie, Steve's Contest. *Photo James O'Mahoney*

Rad Ramp LBGP. *Photo James O'Mahoney*

Tom Sims Quiver for an ad. *Photo James O'Mahoney*

Robin Alaway's trademark, the long-leg lift, Long Beach USSA Contest. *Photo James O'Mahoney*

Waldo grits the drop. *Photo James O'Mahoney*

Bahne Team USSA WSA demonstration at the Anaheim Stadium. *Photo James O'Mahoney*

Brian Beardsley's one-foot, nose wheelie at Steve's. *Photo James O'Mahoney*

Steve's Contest, South Bay. *Photo James O'Mahoney*

Gary Hitchcock's Signal Hill Stinger. *Photo James O'Mahoney*

Gary Kocot barefootin' the pool. *Photo James O'Mahoney*

Howard Hood at the USSA WSA Runway
Pro contest. *Photo James O'Mahoney*

Waldo carves back into Mt. Baldy.
Photo James O'Mahoney

Young Herbie Fletcher praising the pipe, Mt. Baldy. *Photo James O'Mahone*

Steve's Southbay. *Photo James O'Mahoney*

Curt Lindgrin's kick flip at Akron. *Photo James O'Mahoney*

Howard Hood's rock & roll runway at the USSA World Pro Contest. *Photo James O'Mahoney*

Bruce Logan sleeping on the nose, LA Sports Arena. *Photo James O'Mahoney*

The Santa Barbara Contest, USSA. *Photo James O'Mahoney*

Gary Kocot, *Skateboard Magazine* Team, 1975 World Champions. *Photo James O'Mahoney*

The Santa Barbara Slalom, USSA. Nice helmet. *Photo James O'Mahoney*

Stevie Monahan. *Photo James O'Mahoney*

Desiree Von Essen. *Photo James O'Mahoney*

Jim Higham. *Photo James O'Mahoney*

Robin Alaway. *Photo James O'Mahoney*

Unk 360-spin air at Steve's. Surf moves might not have dominated because of public opinion, but everything we were as skaters was surf oriented.

Tracy Greene. *Photo James O'Mahoney*

Debbie Eldridge, Performer team.
Photo James O'Mahoney

Michele Matta. *Photo James O'Mahoney*

Donnie Andre. *Photo James O'Mahoney*

Mark Johnson. *Photo James O'Mahoney*

Desiree Von Essen. *Photo James O'Mahoney*

Chris B's Signal Hill World Speed attempt. *Photo James O'Mahoney*

Brian Beardsley at Akron. *Photo James O'Mahoney*

Mark Boden upside down at Akron. *Photo James O'Mahoney*

Infinity Ad. *Photo James O'Mahoney*

Ty Page's Mid-360 at Akron. *Photo James O'Mahoney*

Freeformer vs. White Lightning, Akron, USSA. *Photo James O'Mahoney*

Be Cool, the Vermont Drop. *Photo James O'Mahoney*

Tom Sims, of the *Skateboard Magazine* Team at the Ventura Contest, barefootin'. *Photo James O'Mahoney*

Orange County's Chick Racers. *Photo James O'Mahoney*

Slalom racers at the San Diego USSA World Invitational, Jack Murphy Stadium. *Photo James O'Mahoney*

Little Axle at Steve's South Bay park. *Photo James O'Mahoney*

Jeff O'Mahoney, without helmet, burning the competition at Steve's South Bay, 1975-76 World Champion. *Photo James O'Mahoney*

L. A. Sports Arena slalom.
Photo James O'Mahoney

Steve Monahan's bush dip for a movie. *Photo James O'Mahoney*

Steve's South Bay. *Photo James O'Mahoney*

Hitchcock's model Hobie. *Photo James O'Mahoney*

Orange crates blazing Signal Hill. *Photo James O'Mahoney*

Lonnie Hiramoto stuck to the wall at Steve's. *Photo James O'Mahoney*

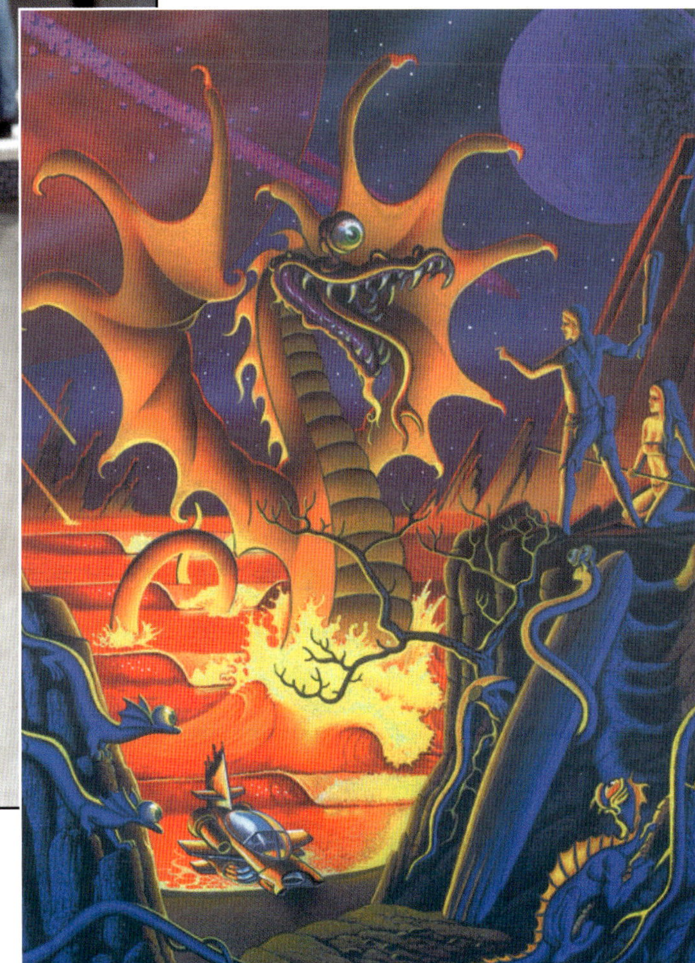

Jim's vision of a possible new world. *Courtesy Jim Phillips*

Stacy Perralta goes sideways at the Runway Pro Contest. *Photo James O'Mahoney*

Hitting the lip at Rad Ramp LBGP. *Photo James O'Mahoney*

Steve's South Bay skate freek-out. *Photo James O'Mahoney*

Wendy on the wall at Runway Pro. *Photo James O'Mahoney*

Beer Boards. *Photo James O'Mahoney*

John Huston's World USSA WSA stand-up speed champion at Signal Hill. *Photo James O'Mahoney*

Howard Hood at Steve's. *Photo James O'Mahoney*

The LB Grand Prix Demo Rad Ramp. *Photo James O'Mahoney*

In the Bowl runway. *Photo James O'Mahoney*

Ellen O'Neil's 2-board Daffy. *Photo James O'Mahoney*

Walk the back, La Costa. *Photo James O'Mahoney*

Jim Higham, no way, Mt. Baldy.
Photo James O'Mahoney

Gary Kocot's Diamond Bar Pool barefootin'.
Photo James O'Mahoney

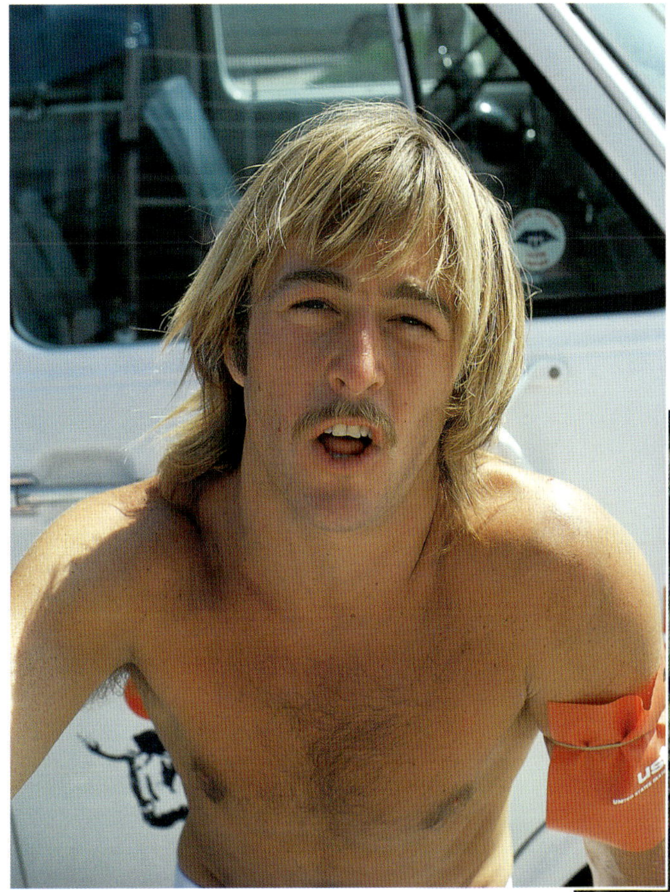

Tom Sims, *Skateboard Magazine* World Team. *Photo James O'Mahoney*

Debbie Eldridge's peace daffy, Northridge USSA Contest. *Photo James O'Mahoney*

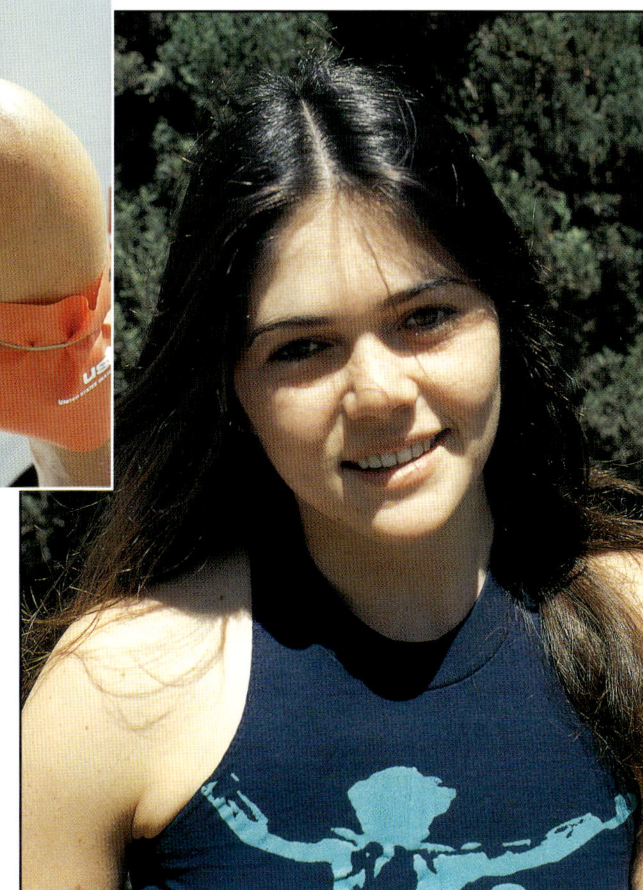

Tina Trefethen, *Skateboard Magazine* World Team. *Photo James O'Mahoney*

La Costa warm-up with Chris Yandell. *Photo James O'Mahoney*

Elephant Brand advertisement. *Photo James O'Mahoney*

Andre's San Pedro board. *Photo James O'Mahoney*

Original X-files skaters. *Photo James O'Mahoney*.

Steve Shipp, Cal Pro. *Photo James O'Mahoney*

Courtesy of Jim Phillips

Magnum Team rider's two-foot nose. *Photo James O'Mahoney*

Power Flex team rider at Akron. *Photo James O'Mahoney*

SS Comp Freestyle. *Photo James O'Mahoney*

Power Flex team rider on a walk up the hill. *Photo James O'Mahoney*

Lonie Toft's board-to-board jump at the Northridge Contest. *Photo James O'Mahoney*

Val Surf Board. *Photo James O'Mahoney*

Andy Priciak, Northridge Freestyle USSA. *Photo James O'Mahoney*

Val Surf. *Photo James O'Mahoney*

Photo James O'Mahoney

James O'Mahoney taking the corner at the Huntington Beach USSA contest. *Photo James O'Mahoney*

Steve's Slalom. *Photo James O'Mahoney*

Val Surf. *Photo James O'Mahoney*

Jennifer Johnson proud in the Santa Barbara contest. *Photo James O'Mahoney*

Photo James O'Mahoney

Wood board, Simms Wheels. *Photo James O'Mahoney*

Steve Shipp with an early ollie.
Photo James O'Mahoney

Steve Brown jumping over Mona Brothers.
Photo James O'Mahoney

Don Andre takes first place honors at Santa Barbara USSA City Championships.
Photo James O'Mahoney

Brian Beardsley at Cal Jam. *Photo James O'Mahoney*

Steve Monahan's Vermont drop multi-image burn, 1975. *Photo James O'Mahoney*

Jim O'Mahoney with an ice power slide. *Photo by Maldinado. Courtesy of James O Mahoney*

Palos Verdes' Pirate Bowl. *Photo James O'Mahoney*

Kenny Means on his specialized kneeboard. *Photo James O'Mahoney*

Courtesy Jim Phillips

Saddleback Hills competition. *Courtesy of Leroy Grannis*

Courtesy of Leroy Grannis

Courtesy of Leroy Grannis

Downhill switchback at Saddleback Hills. Boy, they sure don't make them like they used to. *Courtesy of Leroy Grannis*

Leroy Grannis. You can't say enough good about this great surf and skate photographer. He is truly an icon. *Photo R. Noll*

Slalom run at Saddleback. *Courtesy of Leroy Grannis*

Groovin' in the '70s. *Courtesy of Leroy Grannis*

Saddleback Reservoir. *Courtesy of Leroy Grannis*

This is where I grew up, Hermose Beach pier, from PV to Manhattan. That was my stomping ground. In fact, I keep looking for myself in these photos. *Courtesy of Leroy Grannis*

Courtesy of Leroy Grannis

Courtesy of Leroy Grannis

Some of these Hermosa photos are insane, they truly capture a moment in time. *Courtesy of Leroy Grannis*

Those days on the pier are so gone. *Courtesy of Leroy Grannis*

The old Signal Hill days are over, but speed by no means is. It's alive and well from the luge influence to stand-up downhill. *Courtesy of Leroy Grannis*

Courtesy of Leroy Grannis

Courtesy of Leroy Grannis

Courtesy of Leroy Grannis

Courtesy of Leroy Grannis

The Tale of Skateboarding

Skateboarding has been apart of me my whole life. To tell the tale of skateboarding is to tell the tale of who I am. We had no idea growing up that the sport would explode like it has. It's become a part of our American culture and there's no turning back. I don't see skateboarding fading away in the future, in fact my prediction is for hover boards, you know, anti-gravity boards. Even as futuristic as that sounds, these would still be board sports and will look to us for it's roots or it's history. We are the grandfathers of an amazing legacy that will continue as long as people ride boards.

When I moved to Northern California in the mid-1970s, it was culture shock, to say the least. I was basically a city boy landing in the country. I had just come from the highly skate oriented area of Torrance, California, to a place that was at least a couple of years behind the rest of the world. Back in those days it seemed like I was the only skater in this town. Attitudes in this town were really bad toward skateboarders. People were constantly complaining to my parents that I was out riding that skateboard on the road and were they aware of how dangerous that is! I stuck with it and proceeded to bear my skateboard culture on my pals around town and before long a few locals were joining in on the urethane revolution. We laid down plastic at pier number 5, a cool hill, high on the cliffs of Pebble Beach Drive. Another great hill was Holland Hill, this was a bombing hill. We would skate for speed. I can remember mounting up a water ski, grabbing a football helmet, tightening the trucks down and go. I know now we were going about 35 mph back then. I have ridden the hill presently with a speedometer check. I know its not that fast, but it was to a bunch of pre-teens. I can remember skateboarding was never the path of least resistance with adults. I've been all over this state and a bunch of others, Crescent City remains my home and I am thankful I don't live in the big city.

I personally would like to thank my sponsors. Hotline Wetsuits keep me warm in the cool conditions that I surf in Crescent City. Reef makes the best sole coverage that a skater's foot could ever need. Definitely in the top five soulful companies. Black Fly for covering my eyes and blocking all that harmful UV. Ocean and Earth for board bags that travel wherever I go. Randal Trucks for that safe speed. Priceless!

Steve Shipp jumping over Jim O'Mahoney. *Photo A. Maldinado. Courtesy James O' Mahoney*

Dane Noll and his dad, Rhyn Noll, cruising in Elk Prairie, Northern California. *Photo S. Noll*

360s in the green room. *Photo S. Noll*

Rhyn Noll skating across the old Highway 1, near Santa Barbara, California. *Photo S. Noll*

Sponsors- Reef

Rhyn Noll longboarding in the Ashland, Oregon, park. *Photo S. Noll*

Rhyn Noll at Pebble Beach in Crescent City, California. *Photo S. Noll*

Sponsors- Hot Line Wetsuits USA

Rhyn Noll
Courtesy Attila Aszodi

The New Slalom Racing
by Attila Aszodi

November 19, 2000, the race that changed everything for me took place. Carrasco, Chaput, a guy from San Francisco by the name of Bruce Brewington, Ed Economy, a guy named Brad Edwards (who had never skated slalom before), Mike Gorman, and a guy from Boston named John Gilmore showed up. Twelve racers from all over the U.S.

During practice I heard talk about this guy John Gilmore and that we should watch him, he's fast. I saw John walk up to the top of the hill and do about 15 pushes into the course and witnessed the fastest skating I had ever seen in my life. He was doing a tight course at 25+ mph! It was phenomenal! He was the testament to where slalom had been during the '80s, early '90s, and where it has evolved now. Everybody present was in shock and amazed to see this guy fly down the hill. I had never heard people cheering-on a slalomer like this before. My race began and I ran my first run in over 20 years. I had borrowed a blue G & S slalom skateboard cutaway from Mike Gorman. The setup was with Indy 101's and red Kryptonics classic route 62s. Through the finishing line I fell, landing on my elbow, shoulder and head. To an emergency room I went. My injuries would take me out for about eight weeks. However, I did find out that I still finished fourth, right behind Carrasco, Chaput and Gilmore. Finishing fourth, that made it official for me. I had to race again.

During my period of recovery, I started to work on the new FibreFlex designs. I submitted seven new shapes to Debbie Saili, who ons Fibeflex Skateboard Co., and with the cooperation of the legendary Larry Gordon, in February, 2001. Everybody agreed that one of the designs, the "Response,' should be the first G&S slalom pro-racing model to hit the market. It would also be the first US made slalom race board in over 15 years. The introduction of the new Fibreflex slalom board was announced. So many people around the world had left their skating and FiberFlexes in the past and were pleasantly surprised that Fibreflex was still around and that slalom was still alive. The curiosity was enormous and within a few months G&S classic reissued the "classic slalom and cutaway slalom." Old school Fibreflex had been reborn. Everybody who used to own a Fibreflex wanted a new one, especially since original decks would fetch up to five times the price of a new reissue.

Around the same time a guy named Jack Smith, from Morro Bay, California, announced that the first Slalom National Championship would be held in Morro Bay in May of 2001. The feedback and reaction that came as a result of the announcement was nothing short of amazing. Within 6 weeks more than 40 people registered to compete. The list was now expanding to slalomers from around the world: Germany, France, Switzerland and England. The first Nationals in over ten years was upgraded to become the first Slalom World Championship in over ten years. Over 80 competitors signed up for this event, which was eventually won by US skater Gary Cross from Lake Tahoe. Maurus Strobel, from Switzerland, finished 2nd. This event was the official wake-up call. Slalom was back and people were waiting to get back into it.

With the announcement of the Dogtown and Z-boys movie, Old School was back and in full demand. Old school became the term that would define the new "cool." By the end of 2001, demand and requests for slalom equipment was strong enough to inspire a list of independent entrepreneurs to manufacture components.

Kryptonics brought back the Hyper Strada slalom wheel called the Kryp Grips. Bob Turner came back from retirement to once again lay up his gorm glass marvels. Rick Howell started making Ick Sticks, Tracker Trucks announced RTX slalom trucks. Turner and Chris Chaput, Abec 11, provided large hub slalom wheels and small core large wheels. FibreFlex with four new models and two new signature boards by myself, Attila Aszodi, the Response Pro XL, and the GS Lite.

SSS racing team, from left to right: Richie Carrasco, Attila Aszodi, Chicken Steve Evans. *Courtesy Attila Aszodi*

Team SSS Catalina. *Courtesy Attila Aszodi*

R.O.E racing team. *Left to right:* Chicken, Gareth Roe, Charlie Rarsom, Gary Fluitt. *Courtesy Attila Aszodi*

The course, lit by headlights only, at the Presidio "Battle By The Bay." *Courtesy Attila Aszodi*

Maria Carrasco. *Courtesy Attila Aszodi*

Martin Drayton getting ready in the gates. *Courtesy Attila Aszodi*

The new era of slalom racing was also designed by one more element, Speed! Never before had slalom racing been as fast as it is now, with speeds getting close to 40 mph on very difficult and technical courses. The design of slalom gear started changing accordingly. Decks were wider and longer and stiffer, resembling flat pig-style boards. Wheels grew to be larger with the introduction of Abec 11 Flashbacks at 70mms and the new Turner Avalons at 68mm. No-hubbed wheels are now the official choice as these provide far more speed and rolling power than ordinary 60-66mm large hub wheels. Also, the wider design and lower Durometer rating, 80-85A, provides for maximum traction in Giant Slalom racing.

Chapter 3

The Legends Speak

What sets skateboarding apart now is its brilliant history and its great people.

Duane Peters

Duane Peters, along with Hackett and Olson, is one of the true core racers with a 100% vert background. Having started slalom last year, and within two months already beaten many pros, he exhibits over two decades of racing experience. Duane is part of the vise that makes the current slalom scene one-of-a-kind and reminiscent of the glory days. Duane now rides for Barrett Deck and his "Pocket Pistols."

Duane Peters. *Photo by and courtesy of Attila Aszodi*

Duane Peters at the path. *Courtesy Attila Aszodi*

Rick Howell

Rick is from Upland, California, and is one of the original forces behind the legendary Badlands skating team. In the 1970s and early '80s the team was comprised of Steve Evans, Charlie Ransom, and Curt Kimble. Rick is known for his handmade foam and fiberglass high tech boards, "Ick Sticks." Rick recently resurged and started making boards again after being on hiatus for over 20 years. His board-making skills only improved, providing Charlie Ransom with a winning board at the FCR San Francisco race in March of 2002.

Rick Howell. *Photo by and courtesy of Attila Aszodi*

Skateboards. *Photo by and courtesy of Attila Aszodi*

Rick Howell. *Photo by and courtesy of Attila Aszodi*

Steve Evans

One of the top slalom skaters in the 1970s, "bad lander" Steve Evans reentered the scene in 2001. Etching his way up to the top 10 in the current FCR world slalom series. Sponsored by Rick Howell and his Ick Sticks. Steve remains one of the smoothest and fastest tight slalom racers of all time.

San Francisco finalists: Steve Evans and Mike Maysey. *Photo by and courtesy of Attila Aszodi*

Steve Evans in the finals. *Courtesy Attila Aszodi*

Jack Smith

Jack is from Morro Bay, California is a slalom veteran of over 25 years and achieved some celebrity status in the 70s when he went on the "Skate Across America" tour with team mate Paul Dunn and Gary Fluitt, Bob Danike. Jack's reinvolvement with the sport has opened a new era for slalom racing. In 2001 Jack organized the 1st World Slalom Championship in over 10 years in Morro Bay, California and thus single handedly bringing back organized slalom racing onto the scene. He is also the co creator of the current FCR (Fat City Racing) race series which will close with the world championship in Morro Bay in October of 2002. Jack is also working to reestablish the "Bahne" brand and further the resurgence of the old school phenomenon.

Race promoter Jack Smith. *Photo by and courtesy of Attila Aszodi*

Chris Chaput

Former freestyle world champion and is one of the best all around skaters in the world. He actually has been for nearly 30 years. Currently ranked number 1 in the downhill stand up luge in the world. Chris was one of the few people in 1999 who along with Richy Carraso, Atilla Aszodi, Sean Mallard, Beau Brown, and John Gilmore, helped slalom get the shot of adrenaline it needed to propel to its current status. He is currently ranked in the top 10 in the country and is partners with slalom and race wheel manufacturer. Abec ll which are some of the finest wheels in the industry.

Richie Carrasco and Chris Chaput. *Photo by and courtesy of Attila Aszodi*

Henry Hester

Henry is the champ . In march of 2001, 8 time world champ and legend Henry Hester received an email from Attila Aszodi after listing his famous skate car "White Lightning" on ebay. Attila told him about the upcoming world championship and asked him to get reinvolved with slalom. Henry kindly declined. He ended up being the host of honor at the world championship. After several months of intense training 50 year old Henry proceeded to organize the La Costa Open in Calrsbad California in November 2001. He finished 8th out of 80 racers. Henrys reinvolvement with slalom has provided the current scene with the soul and glamour skateboarding was known for in the 70s. He currently rides his signature board for ROE racing. Beside being one of the best racers of all time, he is a '70s super mogul.

The slalom champ of all, Henry Hester. *Photo by and courtesy of James O'Mahoney*

Henry Hester takes the iron from Mark Downey and Nayo Jaime, USSA & WSA head officials, at Signal Hill World Championships. *Photo James O'Mahoney*

Steve Olson

"Bulky" Steve Olson is currently living in Malibu, California. Few skateboarders in the history of the sport have achieved the level of fame that he has. Steve recently won the La Costa open in 2001. His performance was explosive, proving to the world that he is still one of the finest skaters on the planet. No matter what the event may be.

Steve "Bulky" Olson. *Photo by and courtesy of Attila Aszodi*

Black Leather racing team: Steve Olson, Duane Peters, David Hackett. *Photo by and courtesy of Attila Aszodi.*

John Oshei

John is the brother of race promoter Don Oshei. He is a true downhill hardcore slalom skater. He is currently one of the top guys in GS racing. He rides for Comet Skateboards and is on the Fat City Racing team.

FCR Team Member John Oshei. *Photo by and courtesy of Attila Aszodi*

Russ Howell

Frankly all this fuss about the latest pro is a little irritating when guys like Russ Howell get over looked and unseen. It is my opinion that Russ was one of the first real professional skaters who took what he had to work with to another level. Guys like Russ were at the top of there field, yeah there was a changing of guard but that doesn't change he fact that he and his pals were all doing surf moves and surf skating in the 1960s. What was changing was style and attitude concerning surfing in the '70s and it inundated skateboarding. Because we are surfers, this phenomenon wasn't just happening in one place, it was happening whereever there were surfers skating, and lets face it, this style of surf skating was at the heart of all skaters at this time. When it comes to raw talent Russ kicked ass and was the man to beat. He took so many contests there should be a Russ town movie. Russ pulled up to my house and started pulling 360s and telling me stories of yesteryear and how he fools the kids at his local park, acting like an old guy who doesn't know how to skate. The youngsters might even politely suggest that an injury is inevitable. At that moment, Russ likes to pull some 360 or nose manual; of course the kids are amazed and become interested in Russ's story. Yes, the story we are telling you now is skateboarding history. Russ is one of the guys who made all the work worthwhile. Russ is a super mogul.

Russ Howell Surf Skate. *Photo James O'Mahoney*

Surf Skater Russ Howell demonstrates. *Photo James O'Mahoney*

Russ Howell's 7-board handstand. *Photo James O'Mahoney*

Russ Howell. *Photo James O'Mahoney*

Russ Howell performing tricks with his usual style. *Courtesy of Leroy Grannis*

The Guinness World Record team: Richy and Rene Carrasco at the left, then Russ at Knox Berry Farm in 1978. *Photo Glenn Miyoda. Courtesy Carrasco Family*

Ben Schroeder

Ben is known for his vert skills and technique. He recently picked up slalom and immediately finished in the top 16 out of over 60 racers at the last world championship in Morro Bay 2001. Never having ridden slalom before! He is as unpredictable on the course as capable of taking down the entire regimen of top pros on a good day without any practice.

Ben Schroeder. *Photo by & Courtesy of Attila Aszodi*

Brad Edwards

Brad "Fast Eddy" Edwards is probably one of the most elegant skaters on the circuit and probably one of the fastest. Known for his unbelievable Vert and sliding skills on longboards. Probably the only skater out there who does not skate slalom specific boards and components. He still beats most guys on any given day. A natural born skater.

Brad's "76 pipes." Brad Edwards doing a front-side, Indy grab transfer at a North County, San Diego, secret spot. *Photo Michael Bream. Courtesy Gravity*

Brad cross-step highlands. Brad Edwards cross-step 50-50 in the golden light of Redrock skate park, Highland County. *Photo Michael Bream. Courtesy Gravity*

Brad Edwards and Cliff Coleman come sliding in at dusk, La Costa, California. *Photo Michael Bream. Courtesy Gravity*

Brad Edwards' surf style snap at the Hodges Banks, California. *Photo Michael Bream. Courtesy Gravity*

Laidback Brad Edwards in his final motions completing a front-side five-0 to layback, at the infamous "Kelly's." *Photo Michael Bream. Courtesy Gravity*

Brad Edwards pays respect with a layback slide to the banks that helped many riders of our past become famous, Paul Revere Middle School. *Photo Michael Bream. Courtesy Gravity*

Brad Edwards going back to the roots with some giant slalom at La Costa. *Photo Michael Bream. Courtesy Gravity*

Brad Edwards' rock'n roll, a timeless trick in a new skate park, Montrose, Co. *Photo Michael Bream. Courtesy Gravity*

Brad's snow slide. Brad Edwards mixing it up in the elements. Lay back, snap. Salida ,Co. *Photo Michael Bream. Courtesy Gravity*

Scott Ferrell

Scott is from Modesto, California known for his amazing craftsmanship in modern race board building. With an extensive background and understanding of aircraft construction, Scott builds all his boards entirely by hand and uses exotic materials such as Nomax honeycomb, Kevlar, Carbon Fiber, Aluminum and a variety of unheard of woods that provide his boards with an unmatched finish and feel. Inspired by legendary racers John Hutson and Cliff Coleman he recently entered the racing circuit himself, slowly and evenly working his way to the top.

Scott Ferrell

Michael Bream

Michael Bream owner of Gravity Skateboards decided this year to fully concentrate on racing, grabbing First at the Tahoe FCR race in May 2002. To put things in perspective, Michael still finished in the top 8 in Colorado in June 2002 skating 35 mph with a dislocated shoulder. One of the most respected skaters and movers and shakers in the skating industry, besides a great photographer and a great guy.

Michael Bream at La Costa. *Courtesy Attila Aszodi*

Howard Gordon

Howard Gordon is co-owner of Turner Racing. Bob Turner and Howard created a new and now legendary line up of slalom race boards and components such as wheels and trucks. Since the resurgence of slalom racing in 2001 Turner boards have consistently placed in the top 3 along with riders, Paul Dunn, John Gilmore, Martin Drayton, Floyd Reid, Mike Maysey, and Howard Gordon. Bob Turner boards are as pure-bred and beautiful as they come. Howard Gordon is very active in Turner Racing.

Howard Gordon. *Courtesy Attila Aszodi*

Woody Woodward

Vio Con Dios Ramp
Switch Foot Surf Board Repair

Woody Woodward came to visit while I was at the Carrasco house. This is Woody holding one of the T-shirts from his ramp contest of the past. *Photo R. Noll*

My name is Woody. I've skated since 1963 . I've done a lot with skateboarding and surfing combined. I have taught the history of surfing to a lot of classes at the elementary school level.

In the mid 1980's was the best of my skateboarding experience. I landed in Lake Havasu Arizona, built a forty foot long x 16 x 8 foot ramp. It took some time. I went out and got sponsors locally. They hooked me up. Kids were able to skate for free. I also skated. At 230 pounds, 34 years old, people didn't know what to think. I am 47 now.

Before I sheeted my ramp with masonite this one kid dropped in, slid on his butt and a sliver of plywood 13 inches long went into his cheeks. It came out 6inches after it went in. It missed his muscle tissue thankfully. We carried him into truck, 4 kids with pads and helmets in the back. I couldn't locate the parents, so off to the hospital with them all. At the hospital they got it out, his parents were out to dinner at the time and thanked me for taking care of him all's well ends well.

I have never considered myself a collector. I just enjoy the stuff a lot. I have had this stuff since the 1960s. These old skates are a part of my history and really mean a lot to me. Next to my surfing, I enjoy crusin' on my long skateboard. Now over 40, I keep my butt below my head.

Photos by R. Noll

These are some artifacts that Woody Woodward brought from his collection. *Photo R. Noll*

Woody Woodward is a skate history buff who loves to pass on the history of skateboarding to youngsters. *Photo R. Noll*

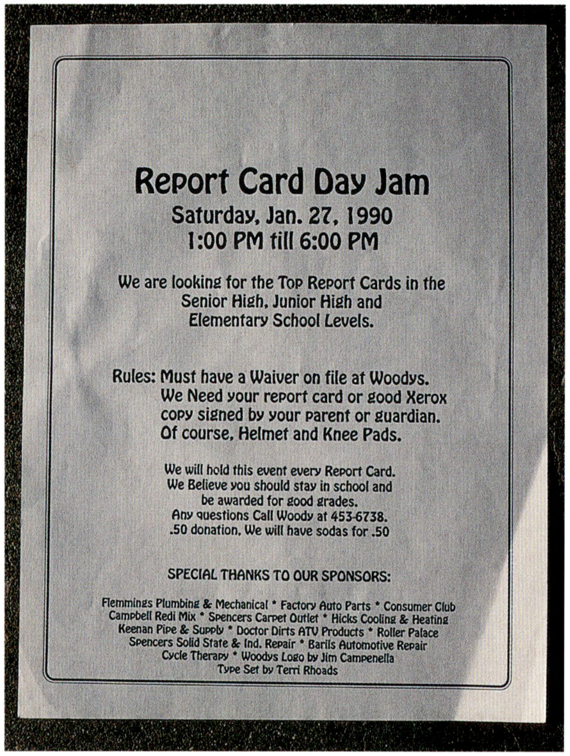

Report Card Day Jam
Saturday, Jan. 27, 1990
1:00 PM till 6:00 PM

We are looking for the Top Report Cards in the Senior High, Junior High and Elementary School Levels.

Rules: Must have a Waiver on file at Woodys.
We Need your report card or good Xerox copy signed by your parent or guardian.
Of course, Helmet and Knee Pads.

We will hold this event every Report Card.
We Believe you should stay in school and be awarded for good grades.
Any questions Call Woody at 453-6738.
.50 donation. We will have sodas for .50

SPECIAL THANKS TO OUR SPONSORS:

Flemmings Plumbing & Mechanical * Factory Auto Parts * Consumer Club
Campbell Redi Mix * Spencers Carpet Outlet * Hicks Cooling & Heating
Keenan Pipe & Supply * Doctor Dirts ATV Products * Roller Palace
Spencers Solid State & Ind. Repair * Barils Automotive Repair
Cycle Therapy * Woodys Logo by Jim Campenella
Type Set by Terri Rhoads

Photo by R. Noll

Photo R. Noll

Photo R Noll

Just a few stickers in Woodie's collection. *Photo R. Noll*

The Flying Carrasco Brothers

Richy, Rene and David are just three in a family of ten boys and five girls. Their folks have been married fifty years. These guys have done it all! Imagine what the rest of the family has done.

All three of the Carrasco brothers: left to right, Richy, Rene, and David, at the 1978 Wild World of *Skateboarding Magazine. Courtesy Carrasco Family*

Renee Carrasco

A man about town. Rene has a heart the size the Los Angeles. A guy with quite a skate legacy to boot . If it's skate related he's probably involved.Rene invited me over to his house and began to tell me a mixed up tale of growing up skating in garden grove in the 1960's. He was telling me about being chased through the neighborhood by a psycho wielding a screw-driver then casually tells of a 1970 encounter with a knife packing psycho in the same neighborhood. Everything eventually mellows out, but is not over by any means. The "suits" at Pepsi decided they wanted a skateboard team. Rene saw the potential and helped to create the Pepsi team. They did demos and contests all over the state of California . In the 1980's Rene honed his skills as a skate boarder, actor, and Tae Kwon Do marshal artist. He is a member of the Screen actors Guild and has a list of 17 television shows, 9 feature films (including being killed by Al Pacino in Scar face). 3 stage productions, and too many commercials too list. Rene also has a certified registered black belt. In retrospect, Rene lived in a house with about ten people, a very large family, and sometimes things got a little hectic. He would grab his skateboard and go out the door, across the street to the hugh parking lot, and skate all his troubles away. When he skated home everything just seemed okay. Rene is a major supporter of the sport and still rips today.

One of the many Plexiglas ramps built in the 1970s. Rene Carrasco is ripping in Tustin, California. *Courtesy Carrasco Family*

Rene Carrasco using two boards as stilts, with hundreds of youngsters looking on, in 1978. *Photo Glenn Miyoda. Courtesy Carrasco Family*

Rene Carrasco started skating in 1960, across the street, in his hometown of Garden Grove, California. He practiced on a homemade roller skate board, leaving a trail of nails down the sidewalk. *Photo Rocky Carrasco*

Rene Carrasco in a double-board handstand. *Photo Glenn Miyoda*

Rene Carrasco holding what he skates now at his house in Garden Grove, California. *Photo R. Noll*

His original Pepsi team board and a photo of Rene riding it.

The smallest actual skateboard I have ever seen. Rene Carrasco uses them for his handstands. *Photo R. Noll*

Richy "360 King" Carrasco

Richy is a classic skater that keeps on clicking he has set the new Guinness world record for consecutive 360s , in the year 2000 with 142 revolutions updated the 1976 record of 35 and a half. Richy has also designed a signature custom 360 wheel, called the Hobie Spinners, marketed in 1979. Richy has performed thousands of skate demenstrations as a member of the Pepsi cola skate team. One of the flying Carassco brothers, he is a hard core skater. He is know for the Carassco brothers backyard skate park. Richy's major contest wins are the guinness world record competion Buena park1978,Vance triple crown ,Slam city jam Vancouver 1998. To name a few . Richy's sponsor's are Vans , Tracker , Oust , and Turner. The Carassco brothers are a tight knit family and all great sportsman.

Rene and his brother, Richy, on the cover of *Longboarder*, 1989. *Photo Maria Carrasco*

The Pepsi team in full regalia. The team photo is a Pepsi promotion. *Photo Carrasco Family*

Rene Carrasco • Age: 26, Team: Pepsi Cola,
Specialty: Slalom, Freestyle Speed

Rene is a multi-talented individual. Not only is he an outstanding skateboarder, having competed in such events as the Southern California Slalom Championships (3rd, Slalom & 3rd, Freestyle), Anaheim (4th, Cross Country), and Escape Country (1st, Downhill Speed), he is proficient in surfing, and has placed 2nd in national karate competition. Rene majored in Art at college and is an award winning cartoonist.

Left to right: Richy and Rene holding what they ride today. Right photo: All-Pro skateboard bubble gum trading card, 1978. *Courtesy Carraso Family*

Richy Carrasco is second from the left, in the back. This is the Powerflex team. *Photo Carrasco Family*

Richy Carrasco's infamous 360 world record board. Notice the engineered 360 wheels. *Photo R. Noll*

Richy Carrasco jumps a longboard while Rene Carrasco assists. *Photo Maria Carrasco*

Photo Maria Carrasco

Richy Carrasco slalom racing in Morrow Bay. *Photo Maria Carrasco*

Richy Carrasco racing downhill in the Carlsbad Mountains. *Photo Maria Carrasco*

Rene and Richy Carrasco's double handstands on the high school path. *Photo Maria Carrasco*

Richy Carrasco on a wild hair day. *Photo Maria Carrasco*

Before ollies, Richy Carrasco was skyhookin' it. *Photo Maria Carrasco*

Richy Carrasco at the Big-O pulling huge vert. *Photo Maria Carrasco*

David Carrasco

He started skateboarding with his brothers, Rene and Richy in 1975 at the age of 14. They practiced on sidewalks, embankments and empty reservoirs. David practiced slalom racing and freestyle skateboarding in front of St. Columban's Church. By age 15 he started entering competitions. The brothers competed in the 1975 Hang Ten World Skateboard Championships in the LA Sports Arena. He also rode for Tiger Enterprises. Then all three Richy, David and Rene joined the Pepsi Skateboarding Team. They did over 1000 demonstrations at schools and shopping centers. David recalls one of the Pepsi Team career highlights of performing in the half time show of the Los Angeles Rams in front of 50,000 people. In 1976 he beat the record that was held by brother Rene for Southern California downhill speed. In 1977 took the Central California Championship for slalom. Set a world record in 1978 for jumping over 9 stacked skateboards. David is married and has 4 girls, while he works for Apple Computers these days.

Tim Carrasco skating while Rene was on the mike, 1978, Plexiglas Pepsi demo. *Courtesy Carrasco Family*

Jim Fitzpatrick

Jim Fitzpatrick's story begins in Point Loma in 1957, where the Wilson family and he built their first skateboards. Jorge P. was the Wilson's patriarch. He had made skate scooters when he was a boy growing up in San Diego, so Jim would basically hound Mister Wilson until Jorge P. would help Jim build his early skateboards. Well, Jim returned back to his home in Bird Rock in La Jolla California and was the first in his neighborhood with a skateboard. He moved to Topanga in the 1960's. Jim's next skateboard experience was a milestone to say the least. He found himself the gremmie hanging around surf guide magazine in Santa Monica where Larry Stevenson, the owner (and to those who don't know, super skate mogul), shows up with a hardwood oak skate deck. At this time Makaha was in its infancy but Jim received an official Makaha deck with clay wheels in 1963. The next thing Jim knew Larry Stevenson gave him 12 Makaha boards which means Jim was a early Makaha Team Rider. Before there were team riders. At the age of 16 Jim went surfing and skating in Europe. He skated in 14 different countries. Jim recalls literally stopping traffic in Paris while he did 360's in the streets and received a French standing ovation.

When he returned to the USA Makaha had formed a team. The Makaha exhibition team. Its members included George Traften, Woody Woodward, Jim Fitzpatrick and Danny Bearer. By 1965 Jim was out of high school. The Hobie and Makaha teams had been firmly established. Jim admits girls were a distraction at this stage of his life and before he knew it.

Jim was married in 1969 and moved back to the beach in 1971. He remembers early urethane wheels and recalls early vert on a home made embankment. Jim's move to Santa Monica in 1975 was a wake up call to a skate boarder out of the sixties, because skateboarding had exploded again. Jim has 2 children at this point and moves to Santa Barbara in 1977. He has lived there ever since. Jim started teaching but he is a journalist at heart and started writing. Later he was employed by the Powell Corporation to edit Bones Brigade intelligence reports. Jim worked with Powell from 1987 to 1994. In that time he witnessed Tony Hawk's rise to fame first hand. Jim was his boss.

In the next stage of his life Mr. Fitzpatrick goes to Washington D.C. Where he set out to change the legislature, that means the laws so that the cities and towns everywhere could have skate parks. The big issue is always insurance and liability claims. To make a long and really complicated story short, Jim went to bat for all of us skaters. He not only changed the way people think, he also got laws that were significant to building and maintaining a skate park changed. To make it even simpler, if it wasn't for Jim

Jim Fitzpatrick cranking a turn back in the 1960s, during the Makaha Team Days. *Courtesy Jim Fitzpatrick*

the skate park you are riding in wouldn't be there. Jim founded the International Association of Skateboard Companies (IASC) in 1995. He had this idea that skateboarders could empower themselves. IASC goal is to successfully change the perception of skateboarding and skateboarders and secure a future for skateboarding with 100's and 1000,s of public skate parks. Jim feels that skateboarders interact and care for the urban environment in a way that pedestrians don't. As for his favorite skate park, "Just about any street" Jim says he is a "transpo" skater now, that means he skates to get somewhere. Jim says his claim to fame is his handwriting and the tour of Europe in 1964 that introduced skateboards to the European continent. From 1962 to 1965 he skated on the Makaha skate team. His skateboard treasure's include a Roller Derby steel-wheeled skateboard and a Makaha clay wheeled board similar to the dozen he took to Europe in 1964.

The irony is I conducted this interview at the Santa Barbara Skate Park and we talked for an hour. Kids skated past, we were ignored for the most part. I was amazed that these kids new so little about their sports history. Here sits one of the moguls responsible for the reason they are there and not one thank you or right on Jim. Well I am here to say "Right on Jim" and Thanks for making future world come true. I think we all owe you a debt of gratitude.

Jim Fitzpatrick at the Santa Barbara Skate Park. *Photo R. Noll*

Left to right: Jim Fitzpatrick, Jim O Mahoney, Scott Star kickin' it on a Santa Barbara evening at the park. *Photo R. Noll*

Tony Hawk

Tony began skating at age 9 and has been dominating competition ever since. That is until he retired. Stacy Peralta says Tony is the first skate boarder who has given the world a face to put on the sport. Tony was voted the coolest big time athlete in front of Tiger Woods and Jordan. Tony's sales with Birdhouse and Blitz is reaching 25 million a year. Bucky Lasek says Tony could put his name on toilet paper and sell it. Tony says his sport is to him exercise expression and its what he loves. Tony makes an estimated 10 million annually and is known by his pals as a Techno Geek. Tony says the goal is to build something that will live beyond my involvement in it. But what you see is what I got. He's done a lot to bring the sport to the next level. Lets just hope that the next level Tony brings us to is soulful at the least and respectful to the history makers all around him in the sport.

An International Association of Skateboard Companies sticker. *Courtesy Jim Fitzpatrick*

Tony Hawk shown giving an award away at his 20th anniversary party, Long Beach, California. *Photo R. Noll*

Tony Hawk seems to be a good dad, here he is performing his duties. *Photo by R. Noll*

Tony Hawk appeasing his adoring fans. *Photo R. Noll*.

Richard Barnick

Richard is 45 years old, married , with three kids. He owns and operates two Surf and Sport Retail Stores. Tsunami Surf & sport in Garberville and Shelter Cove California. Richard has produced and directed over 100 half hour surf, skate, and snowboard television programs on Surf TV, Central Coast Airwaves TV. He has been surfing and skating since 1969. From 1977 to 1980 he was a sponsored semi pro skate boarder. Sponsored by Madrid, Logan Earth Skis and Lickety Sticks. During that time he also managed the Ski Mart Skateboard team while managing a skate park. They used to do demos and exhibitions in Southern California. In 1978 he was part of the pit crew at the Signal Hill Downhill Competition. Has made and acted as a research rider for Madrid Skateboards circa 1978.

While others were braving the neighborhoods in Venice California, Richard was doing it in Compton. In fact he has a Compton story that tells of the standard back yard trespassing for pools. Well one such session he and his crew found themselves amongst the brothers and needless to say they were wondering what was crackin'. To make a long story short, Richard and his pals were crackin'. The coping, that is every time they would grind it the locals were amazed and impressed, the brothers went on their way thinking about the sights. Needless to say Richard and his crew survive the encounter. I think old schoolers like Richard and I can finally be proud of our heritage. We can stand tall and hold our heads high.

A Story by Richard Barnick

You see they were just building the San Onofre Nuclear power plant at the time. Nukes need cooling water, so they manufactured the cooling pipes on the Marine base property.

Good idea, right? Wrong, because a dedicated skater will find a way.

Hurdle #1 was having a base sticker.(Story better left untold as it may be incriminating.) I cannot tell you how petrified we were driving through the base gate being scrutinized, then saluted through. Hurdle # 2 cleared. We could see them off in the distance as we rounded a bend in the road. Rows of them, rows of them, with at least a dozen in each row, separated by 1 to 4-foot gaps. Without a doubt, a pool and piperider's dream-come-true. Remember, its the 1970's. We are talking 18-foot pipes of perfection.

We buried the car in tumbleweeds about a mile from heaven, loaded our gear, and went full stealth. The U.S. Marines wanted our shaggy hair no-rules butts and we wanted those pipes. The Marines meant jail. The pipes meant freedom.

The first couple of runs were pretty scary as skating makes a certain amount of noise. Sha-a-a-aw-o-o-o, Sha-a-a-a-w-o-o-o like a pendulum with wheels. After a while we said to hell with it and started connecting runs through 2- then 3- and 4-sections, each 20-feet long. That's 80 feet of flawless gapped pipeline, "Yee Ha." There were some runs you could get about 10 to11 o'clock up on the wall, at which point the compression would send my knee into my chin, then a short free-fall back to transition. We were riding some of Jerry and Jeff Madrid's first laminate boards. I think they were 7" x 28" with slight ducktail; a huge advantage for vert riders at the time. We shot three rolls of film before the military police caught on. We made it out with great stories of a great session and three photos.

Pipes at San Onofre. *Photo by Pat Egan*

Herb Spitzer, Lee Henderson, and Richard Barnick, the Stealth Crusaders. *Photo Pat Egan*

Shady Acres Skate Park, 1978, North Long Beach, California. *Courtesy Richard Barnick, Tsunami Surf Shop*

Richard Barnick reminiscing in his shop in Garberville, California. *Photo R Noll*

Richard Barnick's personal boards that he rode back in the old days. *Photo R Noll*

One of Richard Barnick's early competition jerseys. *Courtesy Richard Barnick, Tsunami Surf Shop*

The school pool in Compton, California, and a front side grind. *Photo Bob Christiansen*

Jay Adams

His status surpasses most of the hot skaters and, furthermore, what can you say about the guy that hasn't already been said. One thing is for sure his influence seems more powerful now than ever. I think he is one of the first real heroes to come out of skateboardings past. Jay has sole. Jay cares about this great sports history. Jay is one of the greatest skaters ever. He is a mega-mogul.

Jay Adams, Zepher Team, taking the booty. *Photo James O'Mahoney*

Jay Adams doing a timeless surf-style slide in Oahu, Hawaii. *Photo Michael Bream. Courtesy Gravity*

Don Hamilton

Don is 45 years old now and has been skating for 39 years. Don started riding on a red roller derby, in the Verdugo Hills area of California way back in 1962. This deck can be seen in the Skate lab Museum in Simi Valley. In the early 70's he rode with Tony Alva and Stacy Peralta at Carlsbad Skate park, one of California's first parks. In 1975 he was team captain of the Hang Ten skateboard team and competed on ABC's Wide World of Sports with Tony Alva, Stacy Peralta and Ty Page. Don placed in the top 5 of his age group. He has also competed with Tom Sims and Russ Howell. In the late 1970's Don was an unofficial test rider for Tom Sims in a new action sport called "Skurfing". Later this would become known as Snowboarding. It is said that Don was rarely allowed on the mountain but sometimes only if he had a leash.

In 1977 he consulted with Skate park owner Paul Bushnell in the post construction phase of the Boogie Bowl Skate park in Glendale California. Don became the resident pro of the Boogie Bowl skateboard team. He gave safety seminars and taught vert and freestyle classes.

In 1978 Don appeared on ABC's Good Morning America where he shared with million's of viewers the culture of skateboarding, the importance of safety and athletic ability. He released a pro deck model called the DxHx Shredder. Don also appeared in Skateboard World Magazine and the movie called "Spinning Wheels" in the wipe out sequence. During this time he was ranked second best skate boarder in the nation. First was Everett Rosecrans of Vans.

In 1984 Don help build and competed at Jay Moore's Eagle Rock ramp in a series of backyard contests. Then in 1985 he dropped out of the contest scene until resurfacing 16 years later in 2001.

At the age of 42 he breaks his leg in 5 places while doing a 360 rock n roll slide in a 10 foot pool. Then in 2001 Don performed in the 1st Annual old school skate jam, held at Skate lab in Simi Valley. L.A. Access Video sponsored him and at 44 years old Don pulled and landed the "Miller Flip" (360 back flip), 720 revert slide and his trademarked 1978 lay back alley oop air over the hip of the Birch Bowl.

His pride and joy is a 1950's Radio Flyer scooter. Shogoo Kubo Dogtown skate he used to do the first canyon jump in Marina skate park in 1979. His sponsors include Hobie Skateboards, Hang Ten, Lightning Bolt, and Boogie Bowl.

A professional skateboarder shows the *mana* (spiritual connection) that exists between the scooter and the skateboard. *Photo R. Noll.*

Don Hamilton in 1960, at 4 years old. *Photo courtesy Don Hamilton*

Don Hamilton's front side grind, 1979. *Photo courtesy Don Hamilton*

Don Hamilton at an early La Costa, 1976.
Photo courtesy Don Hamilton

The Hang Ten team in 1975.
Photo courtesy Don Hamilton

Don Hamilton at Escondido, California. *Photo courtesy Don Hamilton*

Don Hamilton at Eagle Rock Ramp, 1985.
Photo courtesy of Don Hamilton

Don Hamilton at the B Bowl 1978.
Photo courtesy Don Hamilton

Don Hamilton and his trademark Layback. *Photo courtesy Don Hamilton*

At the Green Thumb Pool Don is over the tile 1989. *Photo courtesy Don* Hamilton

Don Hamilton inverted at the Marina Park, 1979.
Photo courtesy of Don Hamilton

Don Hamilton's front side grab over the gap, 1979.
Photo courtesy Don Hamilton

Here Don Hamilton crosses this gap at Marina, an amazing feat, even today. *Photo Courtesy Don Hamilton*

James O' Mahoney

James O' Mahoney came into this world on August 7, 1945. It seems he was born to establish the sport of skateboarding. He is responsible for many of skate boarding's first's. The first Skate Car was his in 1949 at age 4. James started on a skateboard at the ripe old age of 5. By 1965 he entered the first skateboard competition in Aspen Colorado and placed 1st in Slalom. He also placed 1st at the Maroon Lake competition in the downhill event.

That is just the beginning of his contributions to the sport. He submitted the word "SKATEBOARD" for the dictionary. He published the first skateboarding freestyle trick book. Produced the first World Invitational Skateboard Championships at Jack Murphy Stadium in San Diego. Started the U.S. and World Skateboard Association in 1975. This was the first recognized sanctioning body for the sport of skateboarding worldwide. James Produced the first National Skateboarding Safety Film for the U.S. Library system with Olympic Gold Medalist, Rafer Johnson. James also Established the First Rules and Contest format for all Skateboarding events, U. S. and worldwide. This is the contest kit used by the U. S. Parks and Recreation Service. James published "Skateboard Magazine" in 1975. His pictures were printed by every major magazine in the world.

James established the first world records for skateboarding in Speed-Signal Hill, Barrel Jump and High Jump at Friendship Park in San Pedro California. He produced the skateboarding event for CBS Challenge of the Sexes show with Christy McNichol vs Dan Haggerty (the Grizz). Jim used skateboarding as a launching vehicle for hang gliding in Palos Verde's.

I think James has got to be one of the most influential skate boarders and promoters of the sport. When you look in the dictionary under skateboarding there should be a picture of him. I cant say enough about Jim, his expertise, and knowledge of the sport is unparalled. If he didn't do anything else again and started raising cattle, he will have done more for the sport of skateboarding than some of the bigger name guys that have huge reps. I think he is a hall of fame personality.

James O'Mahoney's first air poster in a French magazine. *Photo by Dryfuss. Courtesy James O'Mahoney*

An advertisement for a Japanese magazine. *Photo by Aki. Courtesy James O'Mahoney*

James O'Mahoney posing as Ronald McDonald. *Courtesy James O'Mahoney*

James O'Mahoney doing a board jump over a four-and-a-half-foot fence, as Ronald McDonald. *Photo by Maldinado. Courtesy James O'Mahoney*

Skater's Point. James O'Mahoney grinding the Taco Bowl. *Photo by Scott Starr. Courtesy James O Mahoney*

Jim O'Mahoney working the obstacles at the Santa Barbara Skate Park. *Photo R. Noll*

Jim O'Mahoney with a 50/50 grind. *Photo by Scott Starr. Courtesy James O'Mahoney*

Jim O'Mahoney with a little power slide, while Santa Barbara shines. *Photo R. Noll*

Scott Star and Jim O'Mahoney getting ready to enjoy an evening at the park. *Photo R. Noll*

Jim O'Mahoney representing his Surf Museum, in Santa Barbara. *Photo R. Noll*

Jim O'Mahoney skates with probably the most recognizable surf board on the planet—it's from the movie *Apocalypse Now*. *Photo R. Noll*

Dave Hackett

Dave has been a legend for over 25 years. he recently got reinvolved with slalom along with Black Leather Racing team mates, Duane Peters and Steve Olson. They provide every venue with as much high caliber entertainment as adrenaline. Dave represents true aggressive and old school style in every sense. He has rapidly moved up in the series to be a major contender.

Dave Hackett at the *Dogtown* premier. *Photo R. Noll*

Dave Hackett chillin' at Catalina. *Courtesy Attila Aszodi*

Rhyn Noll

In the process of running Rhyn Noll Surfboard and Skate Company, I thought it might be fun to build a really long skateboard. Then I thought, why not build the longest skateboard in the world? One of my friends, Jim O'Mahoney, built an 18-footer back in the seventies, but it was basically a wooden beam. They did not claim any record, but it was a starting point: the first longest skateboard. But I wanted to make a real skateboard, no cheating. Anybody could put a kid on a long skateboard, or make a metal board, or put wheels in the center. This to me was chaeting. I wanted to make a real laminated wood skateboard that was 20-feet long.

It took months to plan the perfect design and build a bona-fide skateboard. Thanks to the help of many individuals and companies, the day finally came, May 16, 2002. I was set to ride this thing, not a block or two at five miles per hour, but I planned on riding my 20-foot skateboard at least 25 miles per hour down Howland Hill for at least a half mile. I arrived at the hill to find people everywhere. People in suits and ties, the people officiating and documenting the ride for Guinness World Records, and the media. To say the least, I was nervous.

The officials measured and calculated every aspect of the board right down to the flex. Then the moment of truth arrived. We loaded up the board and started up the hill. Images shoved their way through my pre-ride mental prep, like the board rolling over me and cruching my spleen. Reality was restored when we reached the top of the hill and readied the board for what very well could be the ride of my life.

I proceeded to put on my safety equipment. You have to remember I had never had a 20-foot skateboard up to that kind of speed before, no one had. Then the images were back and this time they brought questions. What if I hit a pebble or a rough spot in the road? Would the trucks rip off because of the long bolts or the weight factor? Thoughts of disaster expelled with one of the deeper breaths I'd taken in a while, and I called for them to close the road.

Everything was silent except the sould of the orange-clad road crew's walkie-talkies. It was as though even the breeze stopped to see what was going on. I had to remember to breathe.

The board was blocked. I prepared to hop into the board, a grove of 100+-foot redwood trees at my back, and a 3/4-mile of 9% grade glaring up at me like the asphalt face of a big wave. I hopped on, and the blocks were yanked away. I had started by descent into hisory.

The world's longest skateboard, 20.25 feet. Rhyn Noll with the Guinness officials. The Guinness World Records Ltd. certificate reads, "Rhyn Noll (USA) built a 6.17 m (20.25 ft) long skateboard called the Super Streetsurfer and rode it for a distance of 1.1 km (0.7 miles) at Crescent City, California, USA, on 16 May 2002."

With all the factoring I had done, it was soon apparent that there was one I had not considered. It's a little-known factor in the performance of a 20-foot skateboard, called torque. My board started to snake out in the back. I was a quarter mile down the hill and knew that if I went down here, it was gonna hurt! I thought, "In five seconds I'm gonna be a tangled blur, wrapped around a tumbling 147-pound skateboard." For whatever unknown reason it only went so far, and then righted itself. Whew! The hardest part was over, although there was still a large crowd at the bottom of the hill. If I lost control of the board at this point, the results could be catassstrophic. I could take out thirty people, including the mayor. So I breathed another gasp of relief when I passed them.

The rest of the ride was fun and then we set up to do it all over, this time a little higher on the hill. The second run went a bit more smoothly, and this time I got my speed up to 30-miles per hour and rode it out 7/10 of a mile. My official Guinness World Record Gold Star Certificate was delivered a few months later. It was definiteily a great experience.

When I rode this thing, it snaked out on me my first run. I thought I was going down. But the board righted itself and I got a 30 mph run.

GUINNESS WORLD RECORDS™

CERTIFICATE

**Rhyn Noll (USA)
built a 6.17 m (20.25 ft) long
skateboard called the
Super Streetsurfer and rode it for
a distance 1.1 km (0.7 miles) at
Crescent City, California, USA, on
16 May 2002**

Keeper of the Records
GUINNESS WORLD RECORDS LTD

www.guinnessworldrecords.com

GUINNESS WORLD RECORDS

www.guinnessworldrecords.com

Rhyn Noll
Noll Surf & Skate
1220 A Second Street
Crescent City
CA 95531
United States

Claim ID: 1758
Membership Number: 1560

25 November 2002

Dear Rhyn Noll,

I am pleased to inform you that you have been successful in setting a new Guinness World Record. A certificate to commemorate this achievement is enclosed.

Details of this record have been entered into our records database for potential use in future Guinness World Records publications and products. Although this certificate does not automatically guarantee an entry our managing editors consider all new records for use as required.

Once again welcome to the very select brand of Guinness World Records holders!

Yours sincerely,

Kat Aalam

Guinness World Records Limited
338 Euston Road London NW1 3BD • Telephone +44 (0)20 7891 4567
Fax +44 (0)20 7891 4501 • e-mail info@guinnessrecords.com
Registered in England, Company number 541295 VAT No.: GB 327 9311 52
Registered Office: Stoneham Gate Stoneham Lane Eastleigh Hampshire SO50 9NW England
A Gullane Entertainment company

Rhyn Noll cutting some trails in a redwood forest.
Photo S. Noll. Courtesy Streetsurfer

Rhyn Noll getting some vert on a 4-foot longboard. *Photo S. Noll. Courtesy Streetsurfer*

This was an incredibly cool experience on a trail in the redwoods. *Photo S. Noll. Courtesy Streetsurfer*

Rhyn Noll with a longboard grind at the Ashland skate park. *Photo S. Noll. Courtesy Streetsurfer*

Rhyn Noll smacking the lip at the Grant's Pass park. *Photo S. Noll. Courtesy Jailhouse*

The Noll family hanging in Klamath, California. *Courtesy Noll family*

Jack Greenbaum

Like me, Jack grew up skating at Riviera Elementary School. He was the Student Body President at Riviera in 1976. Jack can remember when they put the chain across the bowl and they had to start ollie'ing it. Before anybody called it an Ollie. He was younger than the better skaters. Jack remembers feeling intimidated as a pre-teen seeing Laura Thornhill practicing there. Scary teenagers! Skate World, Steve's Super Bowl, Marina Skate Park, "To bad I sucked at vert with all of those good places to skate," Jack says. He lived on Via El Chico below Rocketship Park and got into downhilling. He could bomb the whole hill from top to bottom. In high school Jack crashed a luge board on Ganado Drive at about 40mph and got ticketed by the Police on the same board going down Via Del Monte above Malaga Cove. The judge asked if he was really going 30, and he said "probably not" (he was). He let him go with a $5 fine because he was wearing safety gear and promised not to do it again in front of his mother. He also used to skate all over the Riviera late at night in the summer when he couldn't sleep. Jack doesn't skate much anymore other than checking the surf down the street from his house in Santa Barbara. He put his old Indy 169s and Kryptonics C70s on a longboard so he only has to push twice to make it to the cliffs. Sometimes he will take his fiberglass Bahne with the California Slalom trucks, and wiggle his way there. There is another guy in the neighborhood he sees skating an aluminum Quicksilver (Powell) board that Jack covets mightily.

In an old picture of Jack from the mid 1980's he is sporting some checkerboard Vans. The photo is of an old pool (now gone) in the Santa Barbara foothills called "The Fly Bowl." They used to go there instead of classes in his college days.

Jack Greenbaum. *Courtesy of Jack Greenbaum*

Gene Cooper

"They used to have this grinder to take the rocks out of your wheels so you could go into the roller rink. In those days, everybody had a board, everybody made one in wood shop."

Gene lives in Grants Pass now and started skating back in the 1960's. He did exhibitions at the cow Palace in San Francisco and the Leroy Home for boys. Jumping the hurdles-to see who could jump the highest. You could either send your board underneath and land it on the other side, or jump from one board to another says Gene.

Gene refers to his group of skaters as the San Gabriel Valley Skateboarders. We skated more cement than the beach guys did he says, we had nothing to do we had no waves so we surfed the cement. We skated the 10 foot drain pipes. That was the first half pipes skated. Where Up in Glendora, there was the Asuza. These were flood control points, they were run-offs, they all flowed into the L.A. river.

Then they built "Skateboarders Paradise' in Anaheim. It started out with "tin can" beach, then pipeline, and then Wiamia was steeper. At least five or six acres, all cement. The cement was kind of rough. It ended up going bankrupt or something. Then there was the hill up on Laguna Nigel before they built houses up there. It was six lanes wide and it was a mile and three tenths. You had to take up all six lands to make it without going straight and loosing it. Joey Cabelleo and Hobie, all the guys from Dana Point, used to skate up there. Gene is an avid collector of the mini "Tech Deck." These boards are released in generation series sets of 6. They are full graphics and pro riders replicas in mini. They have potential as far as collectability. Well I don't know if this all of them but its more than any sane man could deal with. I guess when it comes to collectables only time tells whose crazy or crazy like a fox.

Gene Cooper. *Photo R. Noll*

Gene Cooper pulling 360s in Grants Pass, Oregon. *Photo. R. Noll*

Gene Cooper and his collection of Tech Decks. *Photo R. Noll.*

Buddy Carr

Buddy is co-owner of Tracker Trucks with Linda Prettyman. He is 35 years old and lives in Carlsbad California. He was born in Dayton, Ohio and skates about 4 times a month these days. He likes the skate parks in Fontana, Vans Orange County, Coronado and Clairmont. As far as street skating he goes from the parking lot to the pool and the only thing he likes to hit on the street is smooth concrete. Buddy feels fortunate to have skated with Alva Skateboards, riding pools with Tony Alva, Duncan Delgado, and the rest of the Alva team or the Alva posse as he calls them. That was back in the late 1980's, now in 2002 he still skates with Tony and some of his old Alva teammates. Buddy says back then we rode skateboards to stand out, not to fit in now it seems the tide has switched. Skateboarding is a strange thing, almost a virus type organism that infects some of us so much that we build a life around it. He is glad that he was infected many years ago and still has the bug and it will go to the grave with him. Skating has allowed him to meet so many really great, creative and sincere people in pools and now behind the desk as a skateboard manufacturer. Buddy recalls his first rip to Germany back in the 1980's when he got off of the plane he didn't know anyone but he knew if he could find the local skate spots the locals would be more than happy to help a fellow skate boarder. You have to remember that skateboarding wasn't the mega sport it is today. There wasn't a skater on every corner so it made the skate comrade thing even stronger. We were outcasts among the masses at that time. My skateboard has taken me around the world to so many countries and still does to this day. Its funny to think that doing something you love can actually take you to crazy places. I am truly fortunate to have the friends and memories formed through out the years.

Buddy has a small collection of skate equipment and says his favorite all time board is the hand stripped 1960's era steel wheel cruiser that Ed Roth stripped for him before his recent death.

Tracker was founded in 1975 by Larry Balma. Buddy started at Tracker Trucks in 1985 basically his job was taking the rough edges off of the hangers by using a grinding belt. He moved onto other parts of the hands on operations and 17 years later Buddy, Larry and Linda control all aspects of the daily operations. Tracker Trucks was the first production skateboard truck ever. All trucks are basically just modifications of what Tracker produced in 1975. Tracker is truly the original skate truck and the others, some good and some bad, all use Trackers basic idea. If there was a family tree drawing, Tracker would be at the beginning and all others would grow from the original Tracker seed, says Buddy.

Tracker Trucks has a very active skate team with members in France, Germany, Canada, and the USA. Various members are at contests nearly every weekend of the year.

Buddy Carr from Tracker Truck,s outside the *Dogtown* premier in Southern California. *Photo R. Noll*

Atilla Aszodi

My first skateboard was a yellow fiberglass "Sidewinder" with ACS trucks and some clear urethane wheels with loose ball bearings. Little did I know that this crappy little thing would eventually have me hooked and committed for life. That was the early 1970s in Germany. Within the next few years, skateboard competition would become the lifeline that would inspire me to eventually move to California in 1984. In 1977, competitive skateboarding in Europe consisted primarily of 4 major disciplines. Freestyle, Slalom, High jump and Long jump. Although Ramp and Vert skating became immensely popular in Europe in the late 1970s and early 80's, it was Freestyle and Slalom that kept skateboarding alive to date. Freestyle was primarily inspired by Rocco and Muellen and Slalom had Hester and Hutson as their champions. Thanks to Skateboarder Magazine, this California Dreaming would result in numerous European defections to California, including mine.

The name to be proud of was Fiberflex, by Gordon and Smith. The feel was right, the finish and look were without compare. In 1981 after competing at Del Mar in my last freestyle (against Primo and Muellen), I sold my priceless skate collection at a German flea market of $35 and decided to grow up and get involved in showbiz. In 1984 after serving my civil service in Germany, I moved to L.A. and got a fraction closer to this dream. Sadly skateboarding was the last thing on my mind. The scene was too aggressive, too much anger with no style. That in a sense was my official retiring from the board.

Over the next 16 years, I would make a living as a painter, actor, propman, set decorator, and photographer, the latter being his current job. He never looked back to his past or what had brought him to America originally. Everything seemed in place and perfectly adjusted. Still, the feeling to tap into the wildfire of the past, whether it'd be skating or living the simple life, always seemed to creep up once in a while.

I got started again in 1999 by driving by a skate shop in the valley and noticed a long cruiser in the window. I was drawn to it immediately because of its resemblance to the Fiberflex boards, except this one was quite a bit bigger. I went ahead and paid the $135 for it and the board became a project. I wanted to meet people who would ride this type of board, soft and flexy, turny trucks, laminate construction. I went on e-bay and did a name search under "skateboard" and was amazed at the world that had quietly existed in the collectors circle! By narrowing my search down to "Fiberflex," I ended up finding a G & S longboard for $80 which I ended up purchasing as well. However, this one (called the "funshape") was different in construction than the originals I remembered from the 1970s, so I continued my search. I would soon find some originals and could not believe that some of these boards went for a premium of $200+, $600, or over $1000 complete. One of the sellers from whom I bought a board told me about the NCDSA and some online retailers. I found a link to Richy Carrasco's website and couldn't believe that he was still skating. Richy had been an idol of mine when he skated in the '70s, unsurpassed in his ability to do 360s. I would learn that Richy actually had gotten better at spinning 360s over the years. I e-mailed and Richy responded right away. Richy told me about some other skaters who are still skating (Chaput, Beau, Primo, Muellen). Then Richy told me about a little slalom gathering that had been taking place then. Richy pushed Attila to show up at the next one. Well, Attila brought his Sector 9 and couldn't even make it past two cones. This was fast and different from Euro courses. After the event I went online and searched for more specific slalom gear: Trackers, Road Riders, etc.

Longskate.com and *Solidskate.com* had a few slalom products at the time, but other than vintage gear on the internet there were no specific slalom components available. I ended up buying several Fiberflex long boards, including a Leemo and set up with Randals, Indies, and Kryptonices, which were great for casual cruising but didn't work for tighter slalom. It became a mission to find the right gear. I ended up finding a link to the Gordon and Smith website. Debbie Saili, Larry Gordon's daughter, was running the shop at the time and within a short period of time we became friends. We shared the same passion for the old school boards of the 1970s and started talking about how cool it cold be to bring some of those old models back. We both agreed that there was something in the air. The right climate and time to push for new slalom products. I told her about the WLAC events and the new slalom vibe. I suggested that perhaps the time might be right for reintroduction of the Fiberflex. She loved the idea and asked me to come up with some designs.

Attila Aszodi of the Fiberflex racing team at Roosters, Irvine, California. *Photo by Chicken. Courtesy Attila Aszodi*

Photo by Chicken. Courtesy Attila Aszodi

Attila Aszodi at the path. *Photo Barnett Deak, a.k.a. Chicken*

Roy Gonzales

In my youth a great transformation was taking place. The older kids who I hung out with, who had once adorned their walls with star athletes and their rooms were full of football, basketball, and baseball paraphernalia, had traded it all for black light rock and surf posters. Their conventional beds were now a mattress on the floor, and next to it were surfboards, skateboards, and an occasional guitar in the midst of this new ambience. They were passing around funny smelling cigarettes! Wow, a lot for a 12-year-old kid to take in! I'd never been so scared in my life and got the hell out of there as fast as I could! My first exposure to the land of hip-dom.

But soon I was drawn back and before I knew it my room looked like theirs and I was begging my parents for a surfboard, skateboard, or guitar! Coming from a low-income family of eight, the guitar and surfboard were out of the question. But my skateboard arrived, and it was like a golden chariot into rebel-riding freedom. First, we were kooks putting carpet on the top and going down hills through cones, until the older guys saw us and laughed and went skating off with style and grace like they had flying carpets. This stylish dance was called "surf-skating," 'cause when these guys weren't at the beach they would be out carving the street like they were riding some endless concrete wave. This was the coolest, so I tried to emulate their moves on my mighty Black Knight. But with clay wheels, and not knowing how to surf, my elbows and knees were never without horrific scabs. But in our crowd, these were war wounds, the bigger the scab, the "gnarlier" you must be. Then, one day, one older guy gave me one of his old skateboards. I knew he did it so he could get in good with my sister, but I gladly made the trade. He had made it himself and had also drawn some monster type graphic on the bottom. Holy shit, nothing was cooler. I instantly became king kook of my kook squad. I knew exactly what to do! My youthful future was clear.

The next year we moved down south, and surfing and skating were my life. There were only a handful of kids that were hip to it. Of course, we all become "A" students in wood shop. We would experiment making different custom skateboards and, me being the artist of the bunch, I'd draw crazy graphics on the bottom and sell them to the nerds who wanted to be cool like us. Between skateboard and bong sales, wood shop was treating me pretty good.

Roy Gonzales. *Photo Courtesy Roy Gonzales*

This is some of the art work that Roy Gonzales has done over the years, in the skateboard industry. *Photo Courtesy Roy Gonzales*

As they raped the landscape around us, they made us a paved playground of hills and driveways and we would ride where no one had before. I started selling my skateboards to Oak Street Surf Shop. I put a kick in the nose to make it look more like a surfboard. My teacher gave me a mold of a water ski and it worked. I showed my new custom board to a couple of guys, they laughed. But one guy turned it around and started riding it backwards and liked it. He could use the kick for his back foot to do 360s. I thought he was nuts but they bought my boards anyway. Oak Street was on the cutting edge of skateboarding. They had the exclusive rights to a new brand of wheels called Metaflex. It was like they came from outer space. Crazy green, red and blue colors, softer rubber type, not like our Flintstone wheels made of clay. When you hit a rock you would stop dead and fly ten feet on the unforgiving concrete that I had become so familiar with. Nobody had them, and if I had reached puberty I would have been laid right and left when I cruised up on chicks with my new custom skate ship. Then came the fateful day that Cadillac wheels arrived. These clear rubber ball-type wonders were to surpass anything that had come before them. State of the art trucks and bearings, these were hot rods next to Model Ts. The box arrived and everyone was so excited! All the older guys were mounting them on their new boards getting ready for the virgin run. When it was time to go all I could do was stand and stare, wishing I could go along. One of the guys handed me a board and said, "C'mon, let's go, but don't blow it, we only got 5 sets." I said, "Heck, no sweat," grabbed that board and flew out the door. Two kicks and I was off. WOW! I was in disbelief.

Me gunning down coast highway with the big guys; Cadillac's maiden voyage. I have never ridden on anything so smooth. I was keeping up, passing pedestrians and parking meters in a blur, and then she appeared. She was an elderly lady, I can still see her face to this day. There she stood, frozen, two bags of groceries and a dog on a leash. I saw my angle and played it, if I could just fly past her left side, past the dog and the shrub, I'd be home free. I made my play, the dog went to take a piss, and I went flying. The next thing I knew I was rolling down the sidewalk and slammed into a parked car. My board had flown onto the coast highway and everything became slow motion. There it sat, motionless. The only things moving were the beautiful golden cylinders spinning in the sunlight. Then, crack, time sped up to 60 mph as a car blew over the board and wheels: wood, trucks, and bearings exploded in different directions. "Noooo!" I screamed. Then all eyes were on me. The lady with the dog, the guys whose car I hit, but mostly the guys. They all screamed, "Ya Kook" in unison. "Go home you little dumb shit." I jumped up, dazed and bloody, and was about to risk my life and run into traffic to salvage the cherished remains when the guy who warned me not to "blow it" stopped me and said, "Just split!" Man, I hadn't felt that low in a long time. So I turned my head and slowly walked home, never looking back, and never to return, until years later. I still skated and got pretty good. Did the pool and park thing, but eventually just stuck to surfing because scabs and saltwater don't mix. I kept up with skateboarding, but mostly on the graphic end illustrating boards for my friends who were not pros. And I watched the third wave of skateboarding blow up to surpass all other board sports. Well, that was my ride though the years, hope you have a good one, too.

Photo Courtesy Roy Gonzales

Photo Courtesy Roy Gonzales

Photo Courtesy Roy Gonzales

Photo Courtesy Roy Gonzales

Photo Courtesy Roy Gonzales

Photo Courtesy Roy Gonzales

Katch!

Katch grew up in Hawaii. He has been drawing since he can remember and has been writing graffiti since he was 12. He loves his wife, painting trains, skateboarding and doing big murals. Katch lived in L.A. after high school to be closer to the things he loves.

He is currently working as the artist and art director of Natural Koncept skateboards. He designs skateboards, wheels, t-shirts, and hats. He also makes all the ads, does most of the filming and works with the team. He has been with Natural Koncept since 1995. Katch listens to hip-hop, reggae, and punk.

Kale Katch Art. *Courtesy Natural Concepts*

Eric Groff

Fish Food Katch Art. *Courtesy Natural Concepts*

One of the original Alva skate collaborators and one of the most respected old school skaters, Eric Groff is as hard-core as a racer, or person for that matter, comes. He is also one of the fastest slalom racers in the United States and draws on his ability to find great lines from his pool and vert expertise. Eric also organized the epic "Old School Skate Jam" and the recent sequel for a one-of-a-kind experience.

John Krisik

John Krisik was one of the original founders of Fat City Racing and owner of Croakies. He is one of the backbones of the current FCR race series along with Don O'shei, and Jack Smith. The series started in March 2002 in San Francisco and will end after 8 races in Morro Bay with the world championship. His influence on the sport are without equal.

Paul Dunn

Paul Dunn's re-involvement with slalom has rised the bar of performance in every sense. He is currently ranked Number One in the coulntry. He has helped Turner Racing to secure a place in the history books by consistently winning. He has placed in the top four of every race he has entered in 2001. Paul is known for his flawless tight stance style and his ability to adapt to any course instantly with minimal practice. His super fast ramp starts make him the most complete slalom racer on the pro circuit. He was the favorite to take the World Championship in October, 2002.

The Catalina Classic, 2002: John Gilmour, Chicken, Paul Dunn, and Steve Evans. *Courtesy Attila Aszodi*

Bob Turner

March 23, San Fransico, Fat City Racing, "The Battle by the Bay" race. During a break in the tight slalom race, Jack Smith announced that the legendary Bob Turner had passed away earlier that day. This news came in the first race of the first official race series in years, during which all Team Turner riders were present. Bob was a true zen master of the slalom scene since the early 1970s. The announcement of his comeback in board making, in 2001, was received with such tremendous enthusiasm that the orders for his new boards were filled immediately. Everybody was thrilled to put down a 50 percent deposit to reserve one of his custom-made masterpieces. Bob's comeback reflected the fact that slalom skateboarding had indeed made a full comeback. It was a testament that this period was about as golden as it had ever been before.

The Turner Summer Ski Heritage of slalom boards always had a special place in skateboarding history. No other boards were as labor intensive and aestethically stunning as Turners. Compared to other boards, Turners were designed to race and not to cruise. They were the only purebred race board on the market. Bob's approach to racing was similar to board making. It takes time to make a good board, just as it takes time to develop a certain style of riding, winning, and being on top. He never gave up on slalom when he stopped making boards. He knew it would resurge. He came back when he felt that the time was right to pick up where he left.

Within a relatively short period of time, Bob Turner drew enough support to help create and establish a new stable of riders. Since his passing, they have ruled the top three spots in almost every event in 2002. The stable included Mike Masey, John Gilmour, Paul Dunn, Martin Drayton, and Dillan Gordon. His reappearance was brief, but Bob was able complete the circle of his love for the sport by giving what many of us have longed for. His impact on the new scene was enormous. The platform he has created for us in the past year will continue to set new standards in racing and slalom board making for years to come. Thanks to Howard Gordon and his family, Peggy and Vince Turner, the legacy will continue. Turner products will continue to be manufactured and will continue to push the envelope.

Team Turner.*Courtesy Attila Aszodi*

Chapter 4

Conclusion

Cory being his showman-self with a backwards grind.
Photo R. Noll. Courtesy Jailhouse

Johnny Edwards nailing it. It looks like an a bomb went off behind him.
Photo R. Noll. Courtesy Jailhouse.

I am grateful that building this book has brought me together with all these bitchin' skaters. Guys like Jim O'Mahoney, Russ Howell, the Carrasco brothers, and the list goes on and on. Meeting these people and talking with them has been a very rewarding experience, even the major motivation for why I did it. I traveled over 10,000 miles in the quest for skateboarding's history. Now I have come to the conclusion. Working through four years of study has lead me to believe that people who participate and contribute to skate boarding's history have soul. They care about the sport's well being and they care about the way it effects them, now and in the future.

I don't know what the "street style kids" of today will be riding when they grow up. I'm of the first generation that has gone back after riding when I was a kid. But it is still a sport of the young. Kids and high school students make up the bulk, but guys like me and many "old schoolers" are riding again. One thing is for sure, the sport has never been so diverse. In reality, I feel that I am just starting what will be a long line of chronicles documenting this sport and its wonderful historical background.

What I don't understand is why some people would *not* want to participate in this project to document skateboard history. Many companies and people I approached did not want to. It was like coming upon the Grand Canyon and not wanting to look at it.

"Street stylers" are rebelling against normalcy. This is America's youth who set the standard, "If it is not supposed to be done, street stylers will try it." If need be, they will break it down and reshape it so that it is workable. That is street skating. In the competitive arenas, obstacles and runs are representative of the street in general. Even ramps are derived from swimming pools and the pool is the backyard; this *is* the street, but not in the purest sense. The closer you get to ramps the more they become vertical.

Rebel, rebel against the ghost in the machine and the ones who don't give a damn about you but only care about the almighty dollars. Rebel. Who are these guys? It's a conglomerate of companies, not just one. It's a conglomerate that has no one who is real at the top. It's the professionals who you can't touch or talk to. They won't give you the time of day. The price we pay for putting these guys on a pedestal is that they become untouchable and callus to history or anything else. Companies, people, and shops make up this industry and this sport. *That's* what's real.

I can almost see it coming, the next change in skateboarding. I'm not sure what to call it, but if you look close enough into the eyes of skate kids you can see the next big revolt coming.

Glossary of Skateboarding Terms

180: One Hundred and eighty degrees. Measure of rotation. Used to describe skateboarding tricks

360: Three hundred and sixty degrees. Measure of rotation. Used to describe skateboarding tricks.

5-0: Grinding with the axle of the rear truck on the edge of the object.

5O-5O: Grinding with the axles of both truck~on the edge of the object.

900: Two and a half revolutions or rotations. Achieved by Tony Hawk in 1999.

A: A measurement for the hardness of skateboard wheels.

ACID DROP: Skating off the end of an object while ollieing or touching the board with your hands.

AIR: When skateboard and skater leave the ground/ramp without ollieing.

ALLEY-OOP: A move in which you turn one way while rotating another.

ARMOR: Your pads.

ANTI-ROCKER: A wheel setup with small wheels in the middle of the skates and larger wheels on the outside. Supposed to allow easier grinds due to the bigger area between wheels.

AXLE: The metal rod running through the hanger, with the wheels screwed on either end.

BACKSIDE: Originated from surfing, the direction you turn if you are traveling up a wave and turn so your back faces the wave. Used to describe your direction of rotation in skating. The opposite of frontside.

BACKSLIDE: A Grind using only the back foot, balancing carefully on the boot and frame.

BACON IN THE PAN: When you wipe out major on a ramp. You slide around and shrivel up like frying bacon.

BANANA: Another term for switch.

BAR: Name for grinding bar or rail.

BANK: An elevated surface, A common urban form of ramp.

BASEPLATE: The flat part of the truck that fixes to the board via four drilled holes for truck bolts. Also has an area to attach a pivot cup and kingpin.

BEARING: The part of the board that bears the friction of movement. There should be two contained within each wheel.

BERANI: A front flip with a 180 in it.

BIGSPIN: A 360-degree shoveit with a 180-degree turn in a backside direction.

BIO: Sideways spin.

BLINDSIDE: A trick where you turn away from the grinding object to grind it.

BLUNT: Going up over an object and landing with the tail along the edge of the object and the rear two wheels on top of the object. The board should then be pointing in a near vertical position.

BOARD: Main platform area of a skateboard.

BOARDWALK: A topside soul with back foot rolling on its toe.

BONED: Pushing the board out in front and pointing downwards in mid-air.

BONELESS: Take the front foot off the board and grab the board with your hand. With you back foot still on the board, jump up. Then place your front foot back on the board and remove your hand before landing.

CAB: Fakie 360

CABALERNO: A backflip with a 180 in it.

CAMEL: Toe-Tap

CASPER: With the board upside down, place the front foot underneath the board and back foot on the tail, pointing the board into the sky.

CAVEMAN RAIL: A rail that is really high and hard to get on.

COMP: Short for competition.

CONCAVE: The contour given to decks. The concave will dip down from the left to right and should be asymmetrical. Provides strength to the board and aids the skater when performing tricks.

COPER: Protective covering for the truck that attaches to the hanger. Protects the truck against grinding.

COPING: Metal piping running along the top edge of park bowls and ramps. Provides a longer life to the ramp and increases the range of skateboarding tricks.

CURB: Concrete up-cropping at the edge of roadways. What coping is to ramps, curbs are to streets.

CURB GRIND: A grind that is done on a curb.

CUSHION: Donut-shaped rubber components found on trucks, slotted onto the kingpin. Provide steering and act as shock absorbers. Can be bought in a range of colors and hardness. Two are needed per truck; the one that's slightly cone shaped fits furthest up the kingpin.

DARKSIDE GRIND: A grind that flips the board upside down; the rider stands on the underside of the board.

DECK: Main platform area of a skateboard.

DELAM: Damage done to a deck through skating as a layer is chipped from the plywood deck. The thin layer removed is called a "delam."

DISASTER: Placing the rear wheels on top of an object with the rail of the board on the edge. The front two wheels are therefore hanging off the object.

DOUBLE ORE-IDA: Vert trick in which you alley-oop 720.

DOWNHILL: Skating as fast as possible down the steepest of hills for the greatest of adrenaline rushes. Has also developed into a separate area of skateboarding with special boards and techniques.

DROP BEARINGS: Loose ball bearings used in the'70s.

DROP-IN: When you enter a ramp from the top.

ELBOW: One mini-half pipe placed at an angle next to another one, allowing you to transfer between them.

EGG PLANT: Hand plant where you plant only the outside hand.

EMB: Embarcadero, San Francisco, America. Once the greatest urban Mecca for skateboarding.

EXPRESS AIR: Grabbing the inside of the skate with the same side hand.

FAKIE: Traveling backwards. Driving a car in reverse is, in effect, "going fakie."

FARSIDE: A grind where you go over the bar and land on the "far side" to start grinding.

FAST SLIDE: A grind using only the front foot.

FAT: Adjective meaning high or far. Used to express a skateboarding trick that is per. formed over a long distance or a great height. Also spelled "Phat."

FEEBLE GRIND: Grinding with the rear truck while the front truck goes over the top of the edge of the object, putting the board at a slight angle to the direction of movement.

FLATLANDER: A skater who skates only street and no vert.

FLIP: Developed from freestyle skating. It involves the board turning upside down in a variety of combinations. A flip is generally considered to be a complete flip over to land back on the wheels.

FOCUS: Snapping the deck into two pieces. It was once "fashionable" to do this when you became frustrated, said to be conjured up by a part of the industry who wanted to sell more boards by making people think it was cool to focus the board they were riding.

FREESTYLE: An area of skating that has now become part of street and vert skating. Used to be performed on low-riding, skinny boards. Tricks consisted of numerous balancing tricks, flips, and shove-its.

FRONTSIDE: Originated from surfing, the direction in which you turn if you are traveling up a wave and turn so you face the wave. Used to describe direction of rotation in skating. The opposite of "backside".

FUN BOX: A platform object with banked sides plus a handrail, if you're lucky.

GOOFY: You skate goofy if you skate with your right foot forward. The opposite of regular.

GRAB: Using your hand to "grab" onto your board.

GRAPHICS: The artwork on the bottom of a deck. It helps in telling one deck from another.

GRIND: Moving along the edge or on top of an object with the axles of both trucks.

GRIP TAPE: A sticky-back sandpaper material. Usually black but can be bought in a range of colors, even clear. It is used to cover the top of the deck, to create friction that aids the skater.

HALF CAB: Going from skating backwards to skating forwards.

HALF PIPE: A ramp, usually made out of wood, that looks like half of a pipe.

HANDPLANT: A form of handstand where the board is held in the air either by a hand or feet.

HANDRAIL: Common urban feature, designed for holding on to while traveling up and down stairs, though used by skaters for a whole range of tricks.

HANGER: Part of the truck that gets the most abuse. When you grind, you are grinding along the top of the hanger. Contained inside the hanger is the axle.

HEELFLIP: Flipping the board with your heel. Your front foot should move up and across the board, flipping it in the opposite direction of a kickflip.

HELMET: Protective equipment for your head. Nearly always used in vert skateboarding.

IMPOSSIBLE: Freestyle trick invented by Rodney Mullen. Consists of spinning the board around either foot.

INVERT: Going upside down on the ramp and doing a handstand.

INDY GRAB: Grabbing the board in front of you with the rear hand.

JAM: Getting a load of skaters together for a skateboard session.

K-GRIND: Stands for "Crooked Grind". Grinding along on the leading truck without having the board over the object.
KICK FLIP: Flipping the board by kicking it.
KICK TURN: Rotating on the rear wheels of the board with the front wheels raised from the surface.
KINGPIN: The bolt that holds the hanger, cushions and baseplate together of the truck.
KINK: Used to describe handrails. A kink is the changing of the handrail's angle. A handrail that runs down a set of steps then goes horizontal is a two-kink rail.
LAUNCH RAMP: A portable street ramp made for skaters to launch from.
LIP: The top edge of a ramp.
LIPSLIDE: Sliding along on the rails of the board with the rear wheels going over the object.
MANUAL: What people commonly call a wheelie-traveling along while balanced on the two rear wheels.
McTWIST: 540-degree backside air with a mute grab. Invented by Mike McGill.
MELLONCOLLIE: While in mid-air in an ollie, grabbing the board behind you with the leading hand.
MINI-RAMP: A ramp (two transitioned banks facing each other with flat bottom and platforms) that does not have any vert, usually around 6-feet high.
MM: Millimeters. The standard measurement for the diameter of skateboard wheels.
NOCOMLY: Old-school street skating trick. There are many variations but it basically means to travel along with the rear foot on the tail, then place the front foot on the ground and pop the board into the air.
NOLLIE: Follows the same concepts as an ollie. While traveling along, place the front foot on the nose and pop up into the air using the nose (rather than the tail in an ollie). The exact same as a switch-stance fakie ollie.
NOSE: The part of the deck in front of the front truck. Opposite end to the tail.
NOSEGRAB: Grabbing the front of the board (nose) with the leading hand.
NOSESLIDE: Sliding along an object using the underside of the nose.
OLLIE: Invented by Ollie Gelfand and brought to the streets by Rodney Mullen. Taking air without using your hands. The basis for most skateboarding tricks.
PADS: Protective equipment for the knees and elbows. These are mainly used by vert skaters or and in competitions with insurance worries.
PARK BOWL: A simulated pool or bowl-shaped area in a skatepark.
PIVOT CUP: A plastic cup that fits into the base plate and stops the metal hanger from coming into contact with the metal base plate.
PLATFORM: An elevated flat surface.
PLY: Short for plywood. The most commonly used material for the deck. Usually seven-layer plywood.
POP SHOVEIT: A shoveit mixed with an ollie. Enables shoveits to be performed higher.
PRO: A professional. Someone who gets paid by a company to skateboard. Often has his/her own signature model deck of which he/she has a percentage of the sales.
QUARTER PIPE: One side of a mini-ramp or vert-ramp, but not as wide. Used for gaining speed on a street course or practicing ramp tricks.
RAILS: On the underside of the board, the edges of the deck running along each side of the trucks. They used to be plastic strips attached to the bottom of the board, but now are pretty much built-in.
RAIL SLIDE: Sliding along an object on the part of your board that is the bottom between the trucks.
REGULAR: Skating with your left foot forward. The opposite of "goofy."
REVERT: Finishing a trick coming out forwards, then quickly sliding round 180 to come out backwards.
RIP GRIP: Thin, sticky, back-sponge material stuck to the bottom of boards to give your fingers some grip when grabbing.
RISER: Usually made from plastic or rubber. Fits between the deck and base plate of the truck. Helps absorb shock.
ROCK-AND-ROLL: Ramp trick. Go up to the lip and push the front truck over it. Stall, then turn 180 back down the ramp.
ROLL-IN: To skate along the platform of a ramp, over the lip and down onto the transitions. The part of a ramp that curves onto the platform is also called a roll-in, because of the purpose it serves.
RUBBER: Another name for bushings.
SADPLANT: A variation of a handplant, where your grab the inside rail and straighten your front leg.
SAUSAGE GRIND: Grab your tail while doing a smith grind on your front truck.
SESSION: The act of skateboarding.
SHOVEIT: Turning the board without turning your body, so the board spins round under your feet.
SKETCHY: A term used in dangerous situations, usually meaning unsure.
SLALOM: Zig-zag motion that skiers do, except on hard ground usually with a dedicated skateboard.
SLAM: Another word for failing off your board and hurting yourself.

SLAPPY: Doing grinds along such things as curbs without ollieing onto it.

SLICK: Special plastic layer fixed to the bottom of a deck, supposed to aid sliding.

SMITHGRIND: Grinding with the rear truck while the front truck runs along the side

of the object, not over the top. The center of the board my also be touching the edge of the object.

SNAKE: If you're skating an object in which only a limited number of people can skate, a snake is the person that seems to have more goes than anyone by jumping the naturally occurring "queue."

SNAKE RUN: Twisting path with banked sides.

SPACER: A small hollow cylindrical object, usually made from metal, placed between two bearings inside a wheel.

SPINE: If two ramps are back-to-back and do not have a platform at the point of connection, the upside down "V" shape is called the spine.

STALE FISH GRAB: Grabbing the board behind you with the rear hand.

STANCE: Either regular of goofy. The way in which you stand on your board.

STOKED: The feeling of doing something well.

STREET-SURFING: A traditional old-school approach to skateboarding that emulates surfing style.

SWITCH STANCE: The art of skating the stance that you did not learn to skate with. If you do tricks skating goofy, to skate switch stance you must perform tricks with a regular stance, and vice-versa.

TAIL: The part of the deck behind the rear truck.

TAIL GRAB: Grabbing the rear of the board with the rear hand.

TAIL SAVER: A piece of plastic that attaches to the underside of the tail, designed to prevent wear and tear on the tail.

TAIL SLIDE: Sliding with the tail of the board upon the object and the rest of the board hanging off the object, without having gone over it.

TECHNICAL: The name given to complex skating.

THRASHED: The wear and tear of an object due to skateboarding.

TOSS: Such as "product toss" or "sticker toss". An event usually found at sponsored competitions where products are thrown to the crowd.

TRANSITION: Part of a bank/ramp that inclines in an upward direction.

TRUCK: Fixes to the board, and the wheels fit to the truck. A complete truck is made up of a base plate, hanger, axle, kingpin, cushions, two special washers and two bolts for the axles.

TRUCK BOLTS: Keep the truck attached to the board.

TWEAK: To point the board in a different direction than normal.

VERT: Part of an inclined surface that is vertical in gradient.

WALLIE: Skating onto, up, and over a street object.

WALL RIDE: The act of skating up a vertical wall.

WAX: Used to make objects increasingly slippery for skateboard tricks.

WHEEL SLIDE: The technique of slowing down without putting your feet down. It is what people may commonly call a skid.

WOOD: The material used for decks.

WRISTGUARD: Protective equipment for the wrist. A type of glove containing a plastic/metal splint running along the underside of the wrist onto the palm of the hand.

Resources

Juice magazine. 52 Market, Suite D, Venice, California 90291
Skate Boarder magazine. Surfer publications, Inc. Dana Point, California 92629
Skate Boarder Quarterly. Surfer Publications, Inc. Dana Point, California 92629
Transworld Skaterboarding Business. Times Mirror Magazines. 353 Airport Road, Ocean side, California 92054